THE
3 FINANCIAL STYLES OF VERY
SUCCESSFUL LEADERS

Strategic Approaches to Identifying the Growth Drivers of Every Company

E. TED PRINCE

McGraw·Hill

New York   Chicago   San Francisco   Lisbon   London   Madrid   Mexico City
Milan   New Delhi   San Juan   Seoul   Singapore   Sydney   Toronto

1 2 3 4 5 6 7 8 9 0   DOC/DOC   0 9 8 7 6 5

ISBN 0-07-145429-2

Perth Leadership Institute has applied for trademark for Financial Signature, Perth Leadership Outcome Model, Perth Leadership Outcome Indicator, and Financial Outcome Assessment.

McGraw-Hill books are available at special quantity discounts to use as premiums and sales promotions, or for use in corporate training programs. For more information, please write to the Director of Special Sales, Professional Publishing, McGraw-Hill, Two Penn Plaza, New York, NY 10121-2298. Or contact your local bookstore.

This book is printed on acid-free paper.

CONTENTS

ACKNOWLEDGMENTS

In carrying out the research and writing for this book, I discussed my ideas with numerous people. Many of them helped me just by hearing me out. Most offered comments and advice that also helped me enormously. So many people were helpful that I cannot mention them all, but I thank them deeply for providing that support.

Although he may not know it, Manny London, Professor of Management at Stony Brook University, started me on this journey. He saw a very early version of the ideas presented here and encouraged me to publish them as a book. His encouragement spurred me to do something that I otherwise might not have done.

Professor Murray Low, Director of the Lang Center for Entrepreneurship at Columbia University, quickly assessed the merits of my ideas and encouraged me to pursue them. He provided me with a venue through a seminar I presented at Columbia, and his advice following that event also provided invaluable guidance.

Dr. Cindy McCauley of the Center for Creative Leadership invited me to present my ideas at a colloquium there, which resulted in my taking a somewhat different, ultimately beneficial, tack in my research and writing. The discussions I have had with other staff from the center have helped me to refine my ideas even further.

Professor Henry Tosi of the Warrington College of Business at the University of Florida generously reviewed my first, long manuscript. He, too, felt that there was potential, and I am indebted to him for his encouragement.

I received invaluable support from professor Arnie Heggestad, Director of the Center for Entrepreneurship and Innovation at the University of Florida, where I am a Visiting Lecturer in the Center. In particular, I thank him for helping me to find interns to take part in the research on which some of this book is based.

I must also thank Ron Kirsch and Peter Johnson of the Leadership Development Institute of the University of Florida. They provided valuable guidance and advice to me through a joint program that materially improved the quality of my ideas and writing. I owe a special debt of thanks to Peter Johnson for pointing out many errors and inconsistencies in the early drafts of the manuscript.

My first licensee for the Perth Leadership Outcome Model (PLOM), the proprietary model on which this book is based, was AEG Training of Columbia, Maryland. Its three principals, Jody Camardese, Mike di Giorgio, and John Martin, also helped me improve the overall system through their feedback in our first sessions together.

John Beehner, CEO of Wise Counsel, a faith-based national association of CEOs, was another early licensee as well as a wise person who encouraged me early on to develop my ideas. He also provided a platform of experienced but understanding CEOs who could provide valuable feedback from the field on my ideas and their practical significance.

Two other early clients merit special thanks for taking the considerable risk of working with me at an early stage. Their support and feedback were invaluable to me in improving my approach from a practical, working perspective. One of these clients was Darin Cook, CEO of Infinite Energy, a fast-growing energy marketing firm. His valuable collaboration helped me further develop the Valuation Alignment Program, outlined in the last chapter of this book. The other was Kristin McLauchlan, CEO of Legacy Trust, a fast-growing company in the financial services area. Her willingness to allow me to work with her company and board in some of our first leadership assessments was also invaluable.

By being ready to help me sort out the wheat from the chaff, many of my colleagues in the Perth Leadership Institute enabled me to proceed with a surer step. Neil Voorsanger took the lead in developing our leadership assessments. He not only provided the expertise for a complex and technical field that demands as much art as science, but he also helped out on much broader fronts with advice on strategy and execution of the Institute's programs. His comments on early drafts of the book were penetrating and incisive. Steve Levitt was always ready to provide feedback on the implementation and effect of my ideas. I thank him for the very many practical suggestions he has made, particularly on the client perspectives for our leadership model. Carol Mendoza was a vital resource in the development of our leadership assessments and in carrying out much of the basic statistical research on which this book is based.

Several of my friends also gave me invaluable advice. Tom Soper, an experienced chief human resource officer to several large enterprises, gave me many invaluable insights into CEO and leadership performance that helped me enormously in this book. His many thoughtful comments, based on his in-depth review of the methodological materials underlying PLOM, helped me to clarify many of my ideas. Bill Haldane of Haldane Diogenes, who introduced me to Tom Soper, gave me the benefit of his twenty years of experience in the executive recruiting field. Bill saw the value of my ideas very early on, and his support greatly encouraged me. Jerry Franz also saw the potential of my ideas very early in their gestation and gave me much valuable feedback.

Jeanne Glasser, Senior Editor at McGraw-Hill, provided me with experienced advice that also helped this book reach its final form. I very much appreciate her contributions in this area.

I must record my love and deep appreciation to my wife and family who put up with my crabby moods and familial inattention while I toiled over the book. Terry, my wife, supported me from the beginning despite my ideas being new and untested—and rather risky. I could not have completed this book without her support and love. My son, Douglas, my younger daughter, Jane, and my elder daughter, Becky, all played a huge part in supporting me as well. All of them provided the vital emotional underpinning without which no intense intellectual endeavor is completed.

Of course, I accept all responsibility for any errors, omissions, or misunderstandings that made it into the book. With others, I can say that my work is just one small step in a very large enterprise, and I feel privileged to have played my part.

INTRODUCTION

Why do some CEOs succeed? And why do so many CEOs fail? During a career spent leading companies and observing them as a board member and as a peer, I have seen many CEOs launched and involuntarily retired. I have also seen many CEOs succeed whom everyone had thought would fail. What made the difference between the successes and failures?

Surprisingly, many of the failures I witnessed could not be chalked up to inexperience. Most leaders I observed were sophisticated executives, often veterans of large, successful enterprises, and rigorously selected by their companies for their overall competence, drive, and passion. They had been enormously successful in other enterprises and environments and were fully expected to be brilliantly successful in their new position. But they weren't.

And in the cases of the successes, there were many young and inexperienced founders and leaders; entrepreneurs, both young and old, with stars in their eyes but no experience; leaders sometimes from the wrong side of the tracks, sometimes with little or no education and no business credibility. Yet, against all of the odds, they succeeded.

The problem was one of predictability—we could not predict who would succeed or fail. The standard methods were falling short.

I started to delve more into the problem. How could so many failing leaders exist when they had been hired by such smart boards? The boards were populated by seasoned and experienced businesspeople, investors, shareholders, and other leaders. Wouldn't they recognize a potentially failing leader? Surely their vast combined years of experience and expertise would mean that they would unerringly choose well.

Why couldn't the same boards pick out the up-and-comers? Why were the most successful leaders often those who had thrown off the conventional shackles of leadership?

What about the differences among leaders themselves? Why did a small minority succeed and the others fail? What were the differences between the successful and unsuccessful leaders? How were failing leaders similar?

And the successful leaders were all very competent, intelligent, educated, and driven. What was the difference that we were all somehow missing?

As a board member, I was perplexed as to why, when we hired leaders who were always the most desirable leaders around, who had remarkable, even God-like talents, they were often unable to take the company to the next level, if not beyond.

Then I started noticing patterns, initially very hazy, but then increasingly clear.

I started to see patterns in leaders' personal financial traits. Leaders have widely different approaches in how they deal with money and how they approach the building of value. Top executives have characteristic financial traits, just as they have other traits, such as aggression, drive, and execution. I observed that these financial behaviors were linked to company outcome and to the company's street or market value.

I started to develop a theory of leadership based on this notion. This led to the proprietary model, the Perth Leadership Outcome Model (PLOM), developed and used by the Perth Leadership Institute in its CEO coaching work.

The PLOM is an outcome-based model that bases its criterion for success on how much shareholder value has been increased. If market value increases, the company has succeeded. If not, the company has failed. In this book, I equate outcome with market value.

Identifying a Leader's Financial Traits

I refer to the personal financial traits of a leader as his *financial signature*. This financial signature drives leader behavior in ways that we might not have expected, and it has the potential to explain the financial decisions of a company. It can help us make sense of the company's financial metrics and could be linked with other approaches, such as the Balanced Scorecard. Viewed over time, financial signatures can explain certain patterns of decision making.

Leaders leave an indelible mark on their companies. They leave it through their actions, especially their financial strategies. These telltale behaviors inform us of many things: where the leader is headed, how fast he is proceeding; how much effect his decisions have.

But the financial signature has broader implications for the organization. Along the way, I learned that different types of enterprises have different financial signature requirements for their leaders and top executives. Enterprises at different stages of evolution require different financial signatures. Enterprises in different markets have different financial signature needs. By identifying gaps between leaders' financial signatures and their organizations' needs, we can identify new approaches to optimizing the financial performance of enterprises.

In this book, I identify nine financial signatures. These reveal three different types of financial styles, Surplus, Deficit, and Puzzler, that lead to a number of differing outcomes. The existence of these financial styles forms the basis for this book.

Determining Who Is a Leader

By leader, I mean anyone in a leadership position, at any level. Not just a CEO, but other individuals who lead at the corporate level or at the division or the branch office, or even the unit.

My research has focused on CEOs and those leaders who have profit-and-loss responsibility. But the implications go further than these leaders. The financial signature concept can be valuable to any type of leader, particularly to emerging leaders. Most young executives move into leadership positions without the benefit of any leadership training.

In addition to discussing this new leadership model, I have included self-development exercises targeted at up-and-coming leaders to help them move more surely. I want this book to be of everyday use, for anyone who is a leader—or who could be one.

Tailoring Strategy to Financial Signature and Financial Styles

Conventional leadership approaches imply that good strategies work for any leader. Yet I have observed that management strategies have to be tailored to the particular financial style of each leader to be effective.

If I know the leader's financial style, then I can assess what financial strategies she should and should not use, depending on her unique corporate scenario. These techniques will differ according to the financial signature. My aim is to show how these strategies and techniques should be tailored for different leaders.

Uncovering the Unconscious Financial Signature

Over the years, it has become apparent to me that a leader himself, and, indeed, everyone else around him, was usually unaware of his financial signature and what it meant for the company. It was like a hidden personality that no one, not even the leader, was aware of. This leader, however, was the driving force of the enterprise.

Within the leader were a group of hidden psychological persuaders that drive the leader—and his company—in a particular financial and market value direction. And that direction was not necessarily the one that the company wanted to follow. In fact, it could be one the company specifically did not want.

So wouldn't it be valuable to know about the financial signature of the leader *before* he was hired? This would enable the company to adjust its strategies to his particular financial signature to achieve the best possible outcome.

And wouldn't it be useful if the board knew about its financial signature, too? If it did, the board could tune the running of the company and the composition of its teams so that it had the greatest chance of success.

By understanding leaders' financial signature and style, we can potentially avoid many mistakes and provide them a more supportive environment. And we can hire the leaders who are most likely to succeed.

Rescuing the Accidental Leader

I am a leadership optimist. I believe that many more leaders and senior executives could have succeeded if they had had access to the financial signature concept.

In most cases, leaders are thrown into the deep end to sink or swim with little or no preparation. Most move into a leadership or CEO role without any training. And many later fail.

Most of these leaders and senior executives who fail never knew what hit them. Yet many, if not most, had it in them to succeed—but only if they had been aware of their financial signature. Armed with this knowledge, they could have made the appropriate changes and gone on to succeed.

Recognizing the Limits of the Financial Signature Model

It would be nice to think that the model we set out in this book explains everything about the action-oriented leader. Of course, this is not the case.

There are many other factors that also explain a leader's actions. The work of the Perth Leadership Institute goes well beyond the financial signature alone. In fact, our theory links nonfinancial aspects of leadership with the financial aspects of it. The financial signature is a new construct. But it needs to be overlaid on other such constructs, so that we can arrive at a better explanation of leadership.

Our aim is to add to leadership theory, not to substitute for it.

Methodology

The concepts in this book are based on extensive field-work, including:

- Our work with CEOs
- Our databases of CEOs
- Our pilot and validation studies for our leadership assessments
- Data from our online leadership assessments

Our fieldwork with CEOs encompasses my experience as a CEO for almost twenty years as well as numerous interviews with CEOs and top executives as part of my professional activities. This has provided an invaluable base for this research and its conclusions.

Our research is also based on CEO coaching work through the Perth Leadership Institute. Our clients have provided invaluable feedback, helping us validate the good ideas and discard the bad ones.

Our leadership seminars have also proved an invaluable source of ideas and feedback. These seminars made it clear that the theory had real, practical value to a practicing leader. They confirmed that the financial signature was a new construct.

A key part of the research for this book was the compilation and development of a database of CEOs whom we have worked with over many years. The database includes comprehensive data on some 130 CEOs and has been subjected to extensive statistical analysis.

We have also developed several leadership assessments. The one most relevant to this book is our Financial Outcome Assessment (found at perthleadership.org). Other online assessments, including the Emerging Leader Assessment, the Executive Outcome Assessment, and the Team Outcome Assessment, are also available. Several others are being developed. In developing these assessments we ran several pilot and validation studies. The latter are ongoing and will be so probably for many years.

These assessments have and continue to provide results and new data for our research—and not just in the area of financial signature. This information provides us with different data sets with which to compare our results from our work into financial signature.

Our ongoing research will continue to yield new insights into the concept and impact of financial signature. This book provides the basis for understanding this new, yet practical, approach—one that can inform and improve the financial performance of virtually all executives in leadership positions.

WHAT IS
A FINANCIAL
SIGNATURE?

THE LINK BETWEEN FINANCIAL TRAITS AND ORGANIZATIONAL VALUE

How do the financial traits of a leader affect his company's success? Let's take a look at three different companies with similar leaders in the same market.

Comparisons are frequently made among three media enterprises: News Corporation, headed by mogul Rupert Murdoch[1]; Maxwell Communications, led by his rival, Robert Maxwell; and CNN, with its founder and erstwhile chair, Ted Turner.

All three leaders began with a powerful and similar vision: to build a global media empire. Murdoch's empire was increasingly electronic, Maxwell's was mainly print, and Turner's consisted of a broadcast news network.

These leaders also shared very similar personality traits. They were all extroverted risk takers and powerful promoters bent on acquisition. They also had enormous egos.

Those egos perhaps helped the men the most. From the outset, the trio built corporate empires by leveraging their charm and personality—mainly because they initially had few financial assets on which to capitalize.

Yet only one succeeded and survived as a CEO. What made the difference? Despite their similarities, these three leaders' individual financial approaches led to widely varying outcomes.

Two characteristics help delineate a person's leadership approach: resource utilization and value adding. Resource utilization is a measure of how she spends money and uses resources, while value adding indicates to what degree she aims to add value to the company's products and services. All leaders approach resource utilization and value adding in one of three ways, which we'll discuss in the next chapter.

Looking at one characteristic, resource utilization, of the three leaders in our example, it is apparent that Maxwell and Turner were big spenders across the board. Murdoch was very different and did not flaunt a high-spending persona; he did not spend lavishly solely for personal recognition as Maxwell and Turner did.

The men's degree of resource utilization had a significant effect on the outcome of their companies. In the case of Maxwell, his heavy debt level led to failure. Turner succeeded while CNN was independent, despite heavy spending levels. Murdoch, the lowest spender, relatively speaking, was ultimately able to resurrect his company and its fortunes.

The second financial characteristic is adding value. Of the three leaders in our example, Maxwell clearly added the least value. He was basically a gifted financial engineer and salesperson. Turner was an enormously shrewd financial operator, but he did not expand his empire just by financial engineering. His creation of

CNN was an inspired idea that launched an entirely new media category. Murdoch, too, was an innovator, but his creativity came more from identifying which new trends would take off and jumping on them early in the game than from developing concepts from scratch.

So what did their financial method mean for their companies? Maxwell added the least amount of value to his enterprise. Between his high expenses and low value, there was nothing left to save of his empire, and it failed completely.

Turner added an exceptional amount of value. The CNN leader's high-spending ways were countered by his high value-adding behavior. No matter what the outcome of his spending, there would always be something of real value to keep the ship afloat.

News Corporation's near-death experience came along in the early 1990s. But because of Murdoch's relatively low resource utilization, there were high-value assets to offset the company's debt as long as the company could buckle down and make it work. The company was spared liquidation because of its leader's financial approach.

The difference between Murdoch and Maxwell's empire was not so much their spending habits. Both were similar, although Maxwell's was higher. The clincher was the different level of adding value. News Corporation's edge in this area put Murdoch ahead of Maxwell.

A leader's financial signature has more to tell us about the outcome of *all* of the enterprises that he is involved in as well as about an enterprise's street or market value.

Financial Style and Financial Signature

The two characteristics of financial style that determine a leader's financial signature are resource utilization and value adding. The term *financial signature* represents the fact that these approaches to financial management are reflected in all of the leader's decisions and business strategies. The stamp of the leader's financial signature is evident in everything he does as well as in the financial metrics of the enterprise he leads.

All people have a financial signature, which is reflected in their behavior. As children, for example, it would have shown up in how they spent their pocket money. As they become more experienced, some leaders will become aware of their financial signature and will harness it to their own and their company's advantage. Most leaders, however, are unaware of their financial signature, causing disparities between company needs and their decisions. In many cases, this lack of awareness leads to leadership failure.

Behavior and the Financial Signature

A financial signature is a behavioral imperative, an innate way of dealing with finances. Just as certain personality drivers define a person's leadership style, the financial signature defines her financial style.

All leaders have an inborn calculus for evaluating the risk/reward characteristics and the resource utilization requirements of situations. By identifying a leader's financial signature, we can understand how she evaluates value and resource use issues. This provides an approach to the leader's financial goals and approaches and, thus, to her company's potential market value and potential for success.

The leader's financial signature is reflected in the financial results of her enterprise. Outside observers can infer it by observing the financial metrics of the enterprise. These results can also be used to compare leaders— not only leaders in the same industry but in different industries and in different types of organizations, at different stages of evolution as well.

Significance of the Financial Signature

Knowledge of a leader's financial signature can help improve the performance of his enterprise as well as increase the organization's market value.

Research in this area is limited, primarily because academics have historically argued that a leader has little impact on the outcome of his company, but there has been some. Most notably, a recent article from the MIT Sloan School of Management, "Managing with Style: The Effect of Managers on Firm Policies," has shed new light on the link between the personal profile of the leader and the company's outcome.[2]

Based on extensive research on CEOs and top executives who have switched companies, the authors examine how these executives' managerial style affected the financial strategies of the enterprises they led. Their path-breaking research shows that the personal profiles of top executives have a significant effect on the financial strategy and direction of their organizations and their financial outcomes.

The research in this article supports our own, concluding that the financial outputs of an enterprise as disclosed in its financial statements can reveal the characteristic financial signature of its leaders. What might have been thought of as purely personal characteristics can now be integrated into analysis at the industry and market level.

The financial signature provides a new tool, a novel approach to executive and leader selection, and it establishes innovative benchmarks for more effective company performance. It allows organizations to establish more successful support programs for leaders. It illuminates new paths in the building of and predicting company value.

Notes

1 The author knew Murdoch personally when News Corporation was a shareholder in the company of which he was the CEO in the period 1984–1992.

2 M. Bertrand and A. Schoar, "Managing with Style: The Effect of Managers on Firm Policies" (Working Paper 4280-02, MIT Sloan School of Management, Cambridge, MA, September 2002).

Financial Signature and Enterprise Value

This chapter demonstrated that:

- A leader's financial characteristics—resource utilization and adding value—are a critical factor in the financial performance of the enterprises he or she leads.

- A person's financial signature is innate.

- A leader's financial signature will be reflected in all of his or her financial strategies and decisions.

- Different financial signatures will lead to different levels of financial performance and market value, depending on the leader.

Top Two Takeaways

- Your financial signature is critical to your success as a leader.

- Your financial signature will be reflected in the financial results of the organization you lead.

SELF-DEVELOPMENT EXERCISE

During the last financial year, did your enterprise's financial performance and/or street value:

- Improve?
- Worsen?
- Stay the same?

How was this performance related to your financial signature?

_____

_____

_____

_____

_____

_____

_____

_____

_____

_____

_____

How Financial Signature Affects a Leader's Performance

Some executives are extremely careful in their spending decisions, while others are the opposite. Some enjoy enriching products and services; others deliberately prefer a bare-bones product offering.

As we discussed in Chapter 1, the financial styles of leaders have two distinct and measurable components: resource utilization and value adding. Resource utilization comes down to money, essentially—how leaders spend or conserve it. Value adding deals with the extras companies try to provide their customers, from software upgrades to additional product features to service extras, such as free delivery or guarantees. These two drivers lead to specific patterns of financial performance for the company.

Despite conventional wisdom to the contrary, our research shows that a leader's financial style has a greater effect on an organization's success or failure than other corporate or external factors. Put another way, a leader's financial style is at least as important as the company's product, market, pricing strategies, technology, and strategic plan, and so on.

High/High

Take Case 1 from our database, for example.[1] Case 1 was the CEO of a financial software company. Case 1 had started off in the ranks writing code, then decided to go out on his own and build his own financial system.

Case 1 went public. His company made numerous sales to well-known enterprises and soon became widely known in its field. While it never became the market leader, the company attracted many large companies as its clients.

Case 1 was an extremely bright and driven individual. He also believed that one had to spend money to make money; whether it was sales, marketing, research and development, or even his personal travel and entertainment, Case 1 was usually at the top of the expenses charts. He spent as though his enterprise was a large and successful company, both of which it was not.

On the other hand, Case 1 had also developed a very rich product, and that very rich product had attracted some very well-known names. So on the value-adding driver, Case 1 was undoubtedly up there. He did not stint but was always planning for product upgrades that would provide ever-more features and functionality. Adequate was never good enough for Case 1. If there could be a Mercedes of software products, Case 1 was going to create it—and he almost did.

The problem was the company's high-spending ways. Case 1's rationale for these expenses was that without them he could not attract the high-paying, high-margin customers he needed for business success. The board understood that, but what happened if he did not get them? Would this level of spending drive the company out of business?

In fact, it did. Case 1's company eventually went bankrupt after several years. By that time, two other CEOs had tried unsuccessfully to change the culture of the company enough to solve its many problems.

Case 1 had a high value-adding propensity. But he also had a propensity for high resource utilization. He was a High/High type of leader: high for value adding and high for resource utilization.

This is a recurring pattern in our research. Leaders and top executives with a High/High financial style go in one of two directions. Like Steve Jobs of Apple, they either succeed wonderfully, driven by a rich product and high market penetration, or, like Paul Allen (Bill Gates's ex-partner), they fail.

This particular financial style is great when it works, but it does not work very often. If it does not work, the organization's very survival is at stake.

Low/Low

Of course, not everyone is like Case 1. In fact, some people are just the opposite. Let's take Case 2, who was the leader of a private company.

Case 2, the CEO of a residential fixtures company, came from a retail background. Unlike Case 1, Case 2 was a bare-bones sort of executive. Product features and functionality were not paramount conerns for him. He believed that each product should tightly focus on one particular need and no more than that. In his view, more was worse.

Accordingly, Case 2's products did not need many features, because they were only meeting that one requirement. Case 2 did not spend his waking moments, as did Case 1, trying to figure out how he could improve the product even further. His focus was figuring how to make the product even leaner so that costs could be reduced.

Case 2's financial style was Low/Low: low value adding and low resource utilization. No fuss, no frills.

What happened to Case 2's company? It simply never went anywhere. It did not actually fail; it simply bumped along the bottom, making no money. Case 2's focus on keeping the product lean meant that it lost customers. His lack of spending on the important things meant that there was no investment for sales or service. Customers defected, revenues declined, and, in the end, there was no choice but to close down.

Leaders and executives like Case 2 often end up running an underperforming company. The leader's frugality restricts investments required for building a product or service that meets customer's requirements. If a company like Case 2's does survive, margins are typically low and competition is always a threat. Likewise, its potential returns are limited.

On the upside, such companies do not require a lot of investment. This is not a financial style that will result in a major financial breakthrough in most circumstances. Clearly, this is another financial style whose potential is limited. Bernie Ebbers of WorldCom is a good example of the Low/Low style. The company did so badly that it had to cook its books and make a huge acquisition to hide this fraud.

Not all financial styles are as cut and dried as Case 1 and Case 2. Not all leaders and top executives are high or low on both the value-adding and the resource utilization drivers. Some are high on one and low on the other. In fact, most are somewhere in between. Leaders can and do have a myriad of financial styles that are defined by where they are situated on the resource utilization and value-adding continuum.

The Four Innate Financial Traits

Our research on leaders has identified four fundamental financial traits, based on our two financial drivers. These are:

Resource Utilization
- Frugal (Low)
- Extravagant (High)

Value Adding
- Bare bones (Low)
- Rich (High)

Frugal

Leaders and top executives who are low on the resource utilization driver are frugal. Frugal leaders are just what one would expect; they only grudgingly spend money. They are forever finding ways to cut costs. They watch expenses assiduously and shave investments to the bone. This is the type of leader who expects employees to share hotel rooms when they travel. Sam Walton of Wal-Mart is an example, known for his extreme frugality. Sandy Weill of Citigroup was famous for his frugality, too.

Extravagant

Extravagant leaders are just the opposite. Their expenses are very high in all categories, which is often reflected in high expenses for sales and marketing, particularly in travel and entertainment. General and administrative expenses are high and may include large, sumptuous offices and many assistants. This leader argues, like Case 1, that "one must spend money to make money." Dennis Kozlowski of Tyco is a good example of this type, as shown by the extravagant shindigs he and his wife have thrown. Gerald Tsai of Primerica is also an example of the High/High leader: it took the offer of a private jet service for him to consummate the sale of his company to Smith Barney.

Bare Bones

Leaders with the bare-bones value-adding trait do not believe in "gilding the lily." For them, the job is all about revenue and cash flow in the short term. They are not interested in enriching the product; any money spent on the product is not available for other purposes, such as benefiting the shareholders and improving the balance sheet. Their approach emphasizes that "enough is enough," and they are far more interested in other matters such as sales and customer relationships. Al Dunlap of Sunbeam is an example of this type, as was Eddie Antar of Crazy Eddie fame. Both cut costs to the bone, in fact cutting down into the bone, with huge damage to their companies.

Rich

A rich leader is intensely interested in the product and often gets heavily involved in the details of development. This leader often has a vision of the product and is passionate about it. The vision may even be one with a global or social impact. Bill Gates is famous for focusing on product development. So was Henry Ford. Both these men were personally involved in the design and manufacture of their company's products at an incredibly detailed level.

A rich leader is prepared to forgo short-term benefits for what she perceives to be the much larger payoff in the longer term, often overlooking the costs involved in making that vision a reality.

All leaders and top executives fall into one of these four categories. The different combinations of these personal financial traits and their resulting effect on their company are what this book is all about.

Case Studies of the Resource Utilization Driver

Leaders have different approaches to using the resources available to them, and their resource utilization style affects their company's bottom line in different ways.

Some leaders and executives are more concerned about using as few resources as possible than about anything else. A good example of such a leader is Case 3. He was a High/Low leader—high value adding, low resource utilization.

Case 3 built a group of enterprises in the technology field by keeping his stable of CEOs on a tight leash. Although the CEOs each held that title for their individual company, Case 3 carefully monitored each of their activities, especially their expenses. If expenditures were out of line—in his book, the most heinous sin—they would soon be gone.

Case 3 was legendary for his personal frugality. Although a very wealthy man, he owned only secondhand cars. When he entertained his CEOs, he expected them to pay for the meal out of their own pockets. His attitude to expenses in his enterprise was similar: CEOs were expected to share hotel rooms and to rent the least expensive, compact car when traveling on business.

Case 3, in short, was focused on using as few resources as possible. He believed that there was always a way to cut costs even more.

Case 4 is the CEO of a software company with the Low/High financial signature—low value adding, high resource utilization. Case 4 had come up through the sales ranks of his company. Gregarious, articulate, and confident, he was a superb promoter and salesperson. As CEO, his focus was on leveraging company assets to increase sales.

After being named CEO, Case 4 immediately hired more salespeople, even though this was a huge drain on the company's asset base. He also upgraded his office, replacing all of the existing furniture with expensive pieces more befitting his style. He began traveling more to promote the company and its products, always flying first-class. His style of travel and living was first-class as well. Consequently, the company's expenses rose exponentially in no time.

Ultimately, his lavish spending led to Case 4's ouster by the board. The increased expenses put a significant strain on the company's assets. In the end, it was sold for virtually nothing to avoid being shut down.

Case Studies of the Value-Adding Driver

Leaders have varying propensities to add value to products or services. As with resource utilization, this driver shapes their financial signatures and their potential for success.

Case 5 was the leader of an innovative company that had developed a revolutionary product based on its own proprietary technology. The management team was almost entirely comprised of scientists. Indeed, Case 5, the CEO, had also been one. He was a High/High leader.

Case 5's product was innovative but slow to sell. So Case 5 and his scientific staff devoted themselves to further developing the product. Their sole focus was on product development, despite the fact that customers weren't convinced that they needed the product at all. But Case 5 and his top management team continued to find new uses for the technology, which they continued to develop.

Case 5 had a high value-adding propensity, an internal need to pour his energies and intellect into adding ever-increasing value—at least as he saw it—into his product. His need was independent of immediate market and customer demand for the product. This need to add value was a powerful internal financial trait that manifested itself in the decisions he made about the product and the company he led.

A high value-adding propensity is at the root of our financial system. Many leaders have an innate need to add value. Even though, in many cases, their efforts may never result in commercial success, this does not deter the high value-adding leader.

Unfortunately, a commitment to product excellence does not necessarily lead to success. Far from it. As with Case 1, also a High/High, mentioned earlier in this chapter, a high value-adding propensity can be a recipe for failure. In fact, some of the most successful leaders have a low value-adding propensity.

Case 6 was the quintessential low value-adding leader. The co-CEO of a services company, Case 6 was a bare-bones guy. He did not invest heavily in product or service development because he believed that such investments were inherently risky. Even if the product or service itself was developed successfully, there was no guarantee that the investment would ever pay off. Without a commensurate price increase, the investment could result in a big loss.

In fact, Case 6's personal financial behavior exactly matched his professional approach. He was a Low/Low leader—low value adding and low resource utilization. He was not inclined to making big improvements in anything. His approach could best be described as incremental—and to the extreme. The only basis on which Case 6 would ever approve any type of investment, however small, was if one could prove that the investment would get a very large payback almost immediately. And his hurdle for proof was very high.

Case 6's low value-adding propensity never hurt him or his enterprise. Sure, the company did not create grand products or services that would pay off in a big way. But the company he was co-CEO of always made money. Case 6 is like many leaders with a low value-adding propensity. While they may not have grand visions, their companies usually turn in good profits.

Matching Financial Behavior to Corporate Strategy

Leaders can learn new approaches to financial management; when challenged, however, they are likely to fall back on innate behaviors. Without a stopgap in place, leaders with a high level of resource utilization will revert to their natural inclination toward high spending. Likewise, leaders with a low level of resource utilization are apt to slip back into their frugal ways unless there is a system in place to ensure that the company is constantly investing for its future.

Why is a leader's innate behavior important? In a word, predictability. If we know where a leader stands on each of these two drivers, we know which way he will lean in the absence of intervening forces. In times of crisis or stress, when his normal means of correction do not have time to kick in, we know the approach he is bound to take.

Knowing a leader's financial signature, or innate approach to financial management, provides a tool with which we can predict his company's financial performance. A leader's behavior can provide an indicator regarding a company's preferred approach to creating value.

Measuring the Financial Signature

Our research has shown that the financial signature can be measured by employing just two simple metrics. This approach has major benefits: It reduces the potential complexity of operationalizing the financial signature, and it opens up a new framework for comparing leaders across a wide variety of environments. To begin, first turn to existing and historical financial data.

Public companies are frequently evaluated based on earnings, which is one measure of financial performance. But earnings are a subjective term and can mean different things to different people: operating earnings, net earnings, earnings before tax and interest (EBITDA), and so on. Earnings measures are so subject to spin and interpretation that they are of virtually no use in identifying and assessing an individual's financial signature.

But there is one aspect of earnings that we can use to assess a leader's effect on the company's financial health: the gross margin. An organization's gross margin is the difference between revenues and the direct costs of gaining those revenues. In effect, it is a measure of earnings potential. And the higher the gross margin, the higher the level of value the company possesses. If we know that the leader has been around long enough to affect the company's strategies for adding product or service value, then we have a proxy of the leader's value-adding propensity, the gross margin.

As you will see, we can make extensive use of this metric. It provides us with a tool for assessing one-half of the financial signature of a leader. The data is easily available, as it is a by-product of the normal functioning of virtually every company. Not only can we find data on gross margins for most enterprises, but we can also find it for whole industries. This gives us a basis for comparing leaders not only among organizations but also among markets on the concept of value adding.

There is also a metric, although not quite so clear-cut, to measure a leader's resource utilization: company expenses as a proportion of revenue. Although, like earnings, expenses are easy to manipulate, the term is easily understood and is an acceptable measure of resource utilization.

Throughout this book, we will use the terms *value adding* and *gross margin* and the terms *resource utilization* and *expenses* somewhat interchangeably. In reality, expenses are just a proxy for the concept of resource utilization, just as gross margin represents the concept of value adding.

Notes

1 All of the cases cited in this book are actual, real-world examples, but for obvious reasons each company's anonymity has been maintained.

How Financial Style Affects Leadership Performance

This chapter demonstrated that:

▶ The financial style of a leader is the expression of two financial traits. These are:

   1. The propensity to add value to products and services

   2. The propensity to use more or less resources

▶ A leader's financial signature leads to characteristic financial outcomes for the enterprise he or she runs.

Top Two Takeaways

▶ Whether you are high or low on value adding or resource utilization does not necessarily correlate with financial success for your company.

▶ The financial results of your organization reflect your financial signature.

SELF-DEVELOPMENT EXERCISE

Mark where you are situated on the two drivers:

Value Adding
- High
- Medium
- Low

Resource Utilization
- High
- Medium
- Low

What do you think this might mean for the financial results of the organization you run (or might run in the future)?

_____

_____

_____

_____

_____

_____

_____

_____

_____

_____

FINANCIAL
SIGNATURES AND THE
NINE FINANCIAL
MISSIONS

Although there are an infinite number of possible variations when it comes to a leader's financial signature, like-minded leaders can be grouped into nine basic categories.

For simplicity's sake, the letter *V* will indicate a leader's value-adding propensity and the letter *R* a leader's resource utilization behavior. Each of the two financial signature components also includes a level of intensity, ranging from high (H) to medium (M) to low (L). For example, a CEO with high resource utilization would be represented as HR, while a leader with low resource utilization would be LR. By combining these notations, we can create a matrix of the nine main permutations of a leader's financial signature. (See Figure 3.1.)

The nine types of financial signatures are representative of the fundamental financial strategies that leaders follow. They provide us with a tool to link a leader's financial signature, his or her company's financial performance, and the company's financial outcomes.

FIGURE 3.1 The nine financial signatures.

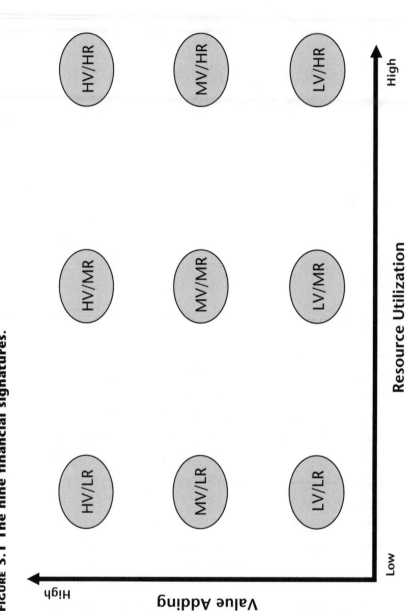

The Nine Financial Missions

The nine financial signatures tell us a lot about the way business leaders view the world. The extent and intensity of their investments in products and services help us identify their value-adding propensities. And their approach to spending and amassing resources gives us a sense of their resource utilization profile. Together, these two components give us a picture of the way leaders view their company's financial goals and strategies.

The nine types of financial signatures possessed by business leaders are deeply ingrained habits. While leaders may take a course of action different from that prescribed by their financial signature, it is difficult. They may become so uncomfortable that, no matter what the external circumstances, they will tend to revert to their innate financial drivers. In theory, they can behave differently; in practice, they prefer not to—even when other choices may appear to be better.

Each of the financial signatures therefore represents a financial preference—a financial mission. The financial mission indicates the particular way leaders' personal financial traits will drive them to create value for their enterprises. It expresses their built-in calculators for achieving profitability.

There are nine financial missions, each corresponding to a financial signature, as shown in Figure 3.2. In addition to the brief descriptions below, Chapter 4 discusses each signature in detail.

FIGURE 3.2 The nine financial missions.

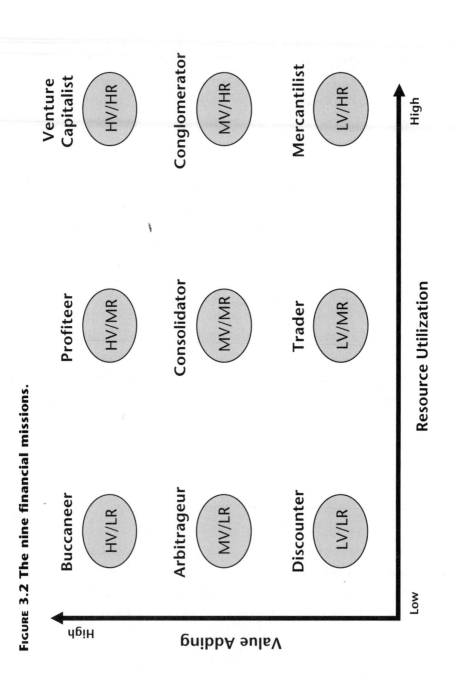

Venture Capitalist Financial Mission (HV/HR)

A Venture Capitalist essentially does things the hard way. He invests in things with high value and gross margins, understanding that it will require high expenditures and investment for several years for the company and product to mature.

If the investment pays off, the Venture Capitalist will reap substantial financial rewards. But in the vast majority of cases, he will fail. This is a risky approach with no easy answers. Whatever he does will require high expenses—there are no shortcuts.

The Venture Capitalist is focused on increasing value in a significant way. To do this uses a large amount of resources. This mission is that of a patient investor who equates long investment cycles with high returns, believing that as long as the company sticks with the investment, he will eventually see high returns from high product value.

Profiteer Financial Mission (HV/MR)

The Profiteer is essentially a cheap Venture Capitalist. She aims for high value adding but without the high resource utilization tolerated by the Venture Capitalist. Instead, the Profiteer shoots for a lower-risk product or service but with high gross margins.

The Profiteer will typically aim for a product with shorter development cycles that provides some cash in the relatively short term, even if that means some reduction in the gross margin. But her aim is to make a lot of money with a high gross margin style, coupled with medium levels of resource utilization; this leader is often a reliable moneymaker.

Buccaneer Financial Mission (HV/LR)

The Buccaneer enjoys very high returns for very low expenditures. Typically, the Buccaneer figures out how to achieve high returns on investment by means no one has thought of before, so he has few competitors.

A Buccaneer will not spend many years developing a product or service; he does not typically have the patience and persistence to do that. He focuses on high gross margins and low resource use. This is a difficult feat to pull off, but some leaders and enterprises achieve it, to the delight of their shareholders.

Conglomerator Financial Mission (MV/HR)

The Conglomerator is a hybrid financial approach that fits between the high and the low gross margin types. Her product is usually not particularly well differentiated, but it is not a commodity, either.

Often, the Conglomerator, as the name implies, has built up a portfolio of products and services, either through internal development or acquisitions. Together these products and services meet the medium levels of value-adding and gross margin characteristics of the signature. However, this approach involves high expenses because of the costs of building the product portfolio, the costs of acquiring the portfolio, or both.

The Conglomerator's financial signature leads to high expenses that are not totally offset by the gross margins the company generates. This is a speculative approach that relies on the balance of the portfolio to generate adequate revenue growth and market share to keep the company in the black.

Consolidator Financial Mission (MV/MR)

As befits his status at the middle of the financial mission archetypes, the Consolidator is a middle-of-the-road, fairly cautious leader. He is not a big-picture thinker or strategist but shies away from cutthroat, low-margin businesses. Neither will the Consolidator make major investments; he invests just enough to keep gross margins up.

As befits the title, the Consolidator consolidates organizationally and productwise. He is not particularly innovative, preferring to add rather than to develop. All of which makes the Consolidator not very exciting, with unspectacular, albeit rather changeable, returns.

Arbitrageur Financial Mission (MV/LR)

The Arbitrageur seeks opportunities carrying decent returns without much risk. She leverages low-cost opportunities so as to make profits on the medium-sized gross margins she will enjoy.

The Arbitrageur is focused on return on investment, but not so much that she will spend more than the absolute minimum to pursue the opportunity. The Arbitrageur cannot be found in mass-market retail or other commodity products; she values higher returns than these areas can bring.

Mercantilist Financial Mission (LV/HR)

The term *mercantilist* describes the economic behavior of nations that use state resources to explore new territories, exploiting whatever resources they may find there. The Mercantilist financial mission represents the leader who uses a high level of resources but is not particularly focused on adding value to products. He may invest in sales and marketing, or in general and administrative expenses, or even in research and development, but not to add any value. The Mercantilist is usually found in a large corporation where the large investments for such speculative and empire-building activities are available as part of the culture.

The Mercantilist looks for ways for high levels of resource utilization to lead to company returns without product intensity, usually by increasing market share. This, of course, is risky. If the high investments do not pay off, the relatively low gross margins reaped by the company are not going to bail it out, and it will have major problems.

Trader Financial Mission (LV/MR)

The Trader is a Mercantilist without the benefit of state backing. Typically a leader in a smaller company who lacks the resources of a big company, the Trader has to pursue projects without much available financing.

Like the Mercantilist, the Trader is low on the value-adding scale, buying low-value products cheaply and selling them for a high-enough gross margin to cover costs and any deficit from her investment activities. The Trader must constantly speculate to ensure that she keeps the two in balance to generate some kind of earnings.

Discounter Financial Mission (LV/LR)

The Discounter is a risk-averse leader who never speculates. His very low levels of added value are offset by extreme thriftiness. The Discounter is generally not focused on adding value to product per se.

The Discounter tends to the details and is very control oriented; he does not focus on the big picture. This type of leader is more concerned about points of market share and gross margin than dominating the market. His emphasis is on lowering resource use to match the gross margin.

What the Financial Mission Means

The nine different financial missions represent nine different ways companies can create value. Each reflects different choices, choices that lead to different financial performance patterns.

Organizations are invariably unaware of the financial signature of their leader or of the members of their top management team. Yet the financial signature drives the entire financial culture of the organization, its financial strategies, and, ultimately, its financial performance. Only by understanding the leader's financial signature can we understand the financial mission.

The Difference Between Financial Signature and Financial Mission

So what *is* the difference between financial signature and financial mission?

A financial signature is fixed. A financial mission is not. A financial signature expresses itself in behavior. That behavior constitutes your financial mission. You cannot change your innate financial signature, but you can change your financial mission and behavior, adjusting them as your experience dictates.

We call compensating for your financial signature by changing your natural financial mission the correction process, which is described in Chapter 7. In addition to showing you how financial missions evolve, we'll also illustrate how most leaders attempt to correct for their financial signature to better match it to their organization's needs. To help you improve the financial success of your own organization, we'll show you what is realistic and what, for many leaders, is not.

Financial Signatures and Financial Missions

This chapter demonstrated that:

▶ There are nine financial signatures.

▶ The nine financial signatures represent nine financial missions.

▶ These financial missions represent nine fundamentally different choices by which leaders attempt to create value for the enterprises they lead.

▶ Financial signature is fixed and innate.

▶ Financial mission is the everyday expression of our financial signature and, although difficult to do, can be changed.

Top Two Takeaways

▶ To understand your financial performance potential, you need to understand your financial signature and your financial mission.

▶ No matter what your financial signature, in principle, you can adapt it to fit your organization's needs.

SELF-DEVELOPMENT EXERCISE

Identify your financial signature by taking the results of the self-development exercise in Chapter 2 and locating their position on Figure 3.1. Write down the financial results for your organization for the last full twelve-month period in which you were its leader:

Gross margin as a percent of revenues_____

Expenses as a percent of revenues_____

Now write down your organization's results for the twelve-month period before you became its leader:

Gross margin as a percent of revenues_____

Expenses as a percent of revenues_____

Did the results under your leadership:

- Increase?
- Decrease?
- Stay the same?

How does this change reflect your financial signature?

_____

_____

_____

_____

CHAPTER 4

THE THREE FINANCIAL STYLES

The nine different financial missions a company's leader can follow can be further reduced to three major financial styles. These three styles are Surplus, Deficit, and Puzzler. All three can be successful in the short term but provide varying results in the long term.

Leaders who have a Surplus style are consistently profitable in the long term. Deficit leaders are consistently unprofitable in the long term by virtue of their financial signature and mission. Puzzler leaders generate zero earnings over the long term, although their short-term results can be all over the board, including being profitable.

Relative Profitability

Let's define what I mean by *profitability* in this book. To compare leaders with different financial signatures and missions, we need to employ the concept of relative profitability—the profitability of an enterprise relative to others in its industry, based on its gross margin and expenses.

Comparing financial signatures means comparing how the gross margin and expenses (on a percentage basis) of a particular enterprise compare to the average levels of gross margin and expenses in its industry. Comparing within an industry helps negate the chance that the financial signature is affected by market fluctuations or the periodic fluctuation of earnings. Once we understand this, we can see how the concept of financial signature provides a universal measuring stick across any type of industry, product, or market.

Let's begin by studying the relationship between financial mission and financial performance.

Financial Mission and the Earnings Gap

A leader's financial signature leads to characteristic patterns of financial performance because, over the long term, a leader will shift the company in the direction of his particular financial signature. The company will thereby reflect the leader's innate preferences in the areas of value adding and resource utilization.

A company's financial performance is determined by the gap between its leader's value-adding and resource utilization styles—the earnings gap. Where the earnings gap is positive, there will be a potential for earnings. Where it is negative, there will be a tendency to losses.

If value adding exceeds resource utilization, the earnings gap will be positive, and the enterprise will generate an operating surplus. If the reverse is the case, the earnings gap will be negative, and the organization will operate at a deficit.

The more positive the earnings gap, the more cash the leader will amass. The cash will fund growth, thus making the company more sustainable over the long term. If the earnings gap is negative, the organization is consuming cash. To make up the cash shortfall, the company may take on debt, find equity capital, or rely on its vendors to tide it over. If there is a sustained level of losses, there will likely be a decline in growth, and the company's viability may become questionable.

For example, if the gross margin of a company is 55 percent of revenues and the total expenses are 45 percent, operating earnings will be 10 percent on the positive side. This is a good outcome for the organization's financial performance. On the other hand, if the gross margin is 45 percent of revenues and the total expenses are 55 percent, then there will be a net operating loss of 10 percent of revenues. Other things being equal, this is clearly bad for financial performance.

Keep in mind that the financial mission of the leader will have an effect on the financial performance of the company over the long term, meaning at least a year and usually much more.

Earnings Gap and the Nine Financial Missions

Each financial mission falls into one of three groups in terms of long-term financial performance.

Positive Earnings Gaps

- **Buccaneer:** this style generates a large positive earnings gap because value adding is high and resource utilization is low, leading to a pattern of fast growth and rising earnings. Sandy Weill of Citigroup and Pierre Omidyar and Jeff Skoll of eBay are examples of the Buccaneer style.
- **Profiteer:** this style creates a positive earnings gap because of high value adding and medium resource utilization, leading to gently rising growth and earnings. Jim Kilts of Gillette is an example of the Profiteer style.
- **Arbitrageur:** this style leads to a positive earnings gap because value adding is medium and resource utilization is low, though growth is slower and earnings increases are moderate. One example of the Arbitrageur style is Rupert Murdoch of News Corporation.

No Earnings Gaps

- **Venture Capitalist:** this leadership style leads to no earnings gap. The leader is high on both value adding and resource utilization, but the company shows an inconsistent pattern of growth and earnings. Growth occasionally spikes but also declines a virtually equivalent number of times. An example of the Venture Capitalist style is Paul Allen of Interval Research, who was Bill Gates's original partner in Microsoft.
- **Discounter:** this style creates no earnings gap. While both resource utilization and value adding are low, growth and earnings are inconsistent. In the short term, there may be periods of apparent survival, but over the long term, death is inevitable. An example of the Discounter style is Bernard Ebbers of WorldCom.

• **Consolidator:** this style also generates no earnings gap. Both resource utilization and value adding are at medium levels, but growth and earnings are inconsistent. The company shows periods of both growth and decline, which average out over the long term. An example of the Consolidator style is Leland Brendsel, the former CEO of Freddie Mac.

Negative Earnings Gaps

• **Mercantilist:** this style creates a large negative earnings gap. Resource utilization is high while value adding is low, which leads to a fast decline in growth and earnings and often to company failure. Dennis Kozlowski of Tyco is an example of the Mercantilist style.

• **Trader:** this style generates a negative earnings gap because resource utilization is medium while value adding is low, leading to a slow decline in growth and earnings. An example of the Trader style is William Clay Ford, CEO of Ford Motor Company.

• **Conglomerator:** this style leads to a negative earnings gap because resource utilization is high and value adding is medium. Declining growth and earnings result over the long term, although short-lived earnings spikes may also occur. An example of the Conglomerator style is Robert Allen's tenure as chair of AT&T.

The Capital Engine

The earnings gap reflects what we call the capital engine, which is the ability of a company to generate cash. The sustained creation of cash allows an enterprise to build capital; the more capital, the higher its ability to invest in sales and products to create company value.

The earnings gap provides the fuel for the capital engine. If there is a surplus, the capital engine pumps out more power. If there is a deficit, the capital engine loses speed. Through this mechanism, the capital engine drives financial performance.

Once we know the financial signature of a leader, we know the earnings gap and the gear the capital engine is in. The three financial missions whose earnings gap is positive—Profiteer, Buccaneer, and Arbitrageur—are profitable long term and power capital engines running in forward gear. For the Mercantilist, Conglomerator, and Trader financial missions, whose gap is negative, their missions are unprofitable long term, and their capital engines are in reverse. And the Venture Capitalist, Consolidator, and Discounter missions that, on average, generate no earnings could go either way. They power engines that are always in neutral.

Figure 4.1 illustrates how the nine financial missions can be grouped according to their propensity to be profitable, unprofitable, or break-even. This does not mean that the financial missions will always prove their profitability or unprofitability if they fall in the appropriate band, but it does indicate that enterprises will be predisposed to fall into one of these performance categories due to the personal financial traits of the leader.

The earnings surplus and the capital engine power all of the financial missions. Over the long haul, companies whose leaders have intrinsically profitable financial missions will make money and increase in market value.

Figure 4.1 Intrinsic profitability of financial missions.

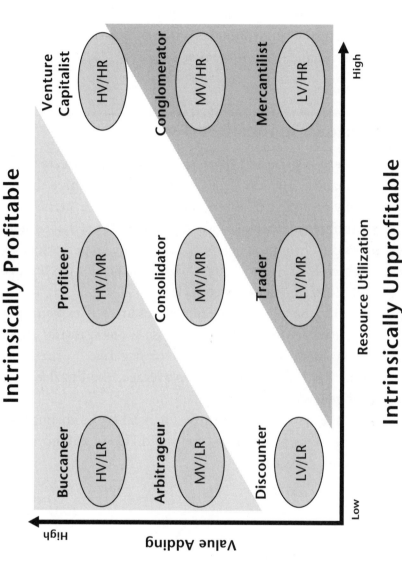

Intrinsically Profitable

Intrinsically Unprofitable

Venture Capitalist — HV/HR
Conglomerator — MV/HR
Mercantilist — LV/HR

Profiteer — HV/MR
Consolidator — MV/MR
Trader — LV/MR

Buccaneer — HV/LR
Arbitrageur — MV/LR
Discounter — LV/LR

Value Adding
High
Low

Resource Utilization
High

And over the longer haul, companies whose leaders have intrinsically unprofitable financial missions will lose money and decline in market value.

Three Financial Styles

As we noted earlier, there are three different categories of financial mission. One category includes three intrinsically profitable missions, one includes three intrinsically unprofitable missions, and one includes three inconsistent missions. From the perspective of financial performance, each category represents a broad financial style. Figure 4.2 illustrates these three styles.

The Surplus and Deficit styles are self-explanatory. The Puzzler financial style is less so, as it results in an inconsistent outcome, positive or negative, in the short term. Over the long term, on average, the Puzzler style will generate zero earnings.

We will use these three financial styles throughout the book as a shorthand for the different categories of financial signatures.

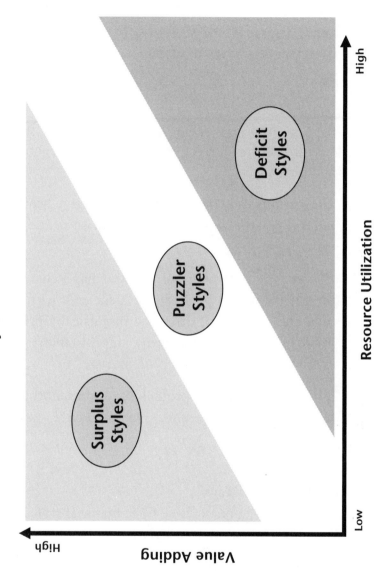

FIGURE 4.2 The three financial styles.

How Financial Signature Drives Enterprise Profitability

This chapter demonstrated that:

▶ The earnings gap between value adding and resource utilization reflects profitability direction and potential.

▶ The earnings gap powers the capital engine, which determines the ability of an enterprise to create value.

▶ Each of the nine financial missions has a characteristic pattern of profitability associated with it: over the long term, three are intrinsically profitable, three are intrinsically unprofitable, and three generate no earnings on average.

▶ The three patterns of profitability represent three basic styles: the Surplus, Deficit, and Puzzler financial styles.

Top Two Takeaways

▶ You will have one of three basic financial styles—Surplus, Deficit, or Puzzler.

▶ This basic financial style shows you the long-term effect of your financial signature on the profitability and financial performance of the organization you lead.

SELF-DEVELOPMENT EXERCISE

Find your financial style from Figure 4.2 and write it down
here.

_____

_____

_____

_____

Write down three reasons why your financial style could
affect the profitability of your organization.

1. _____

   _____

2. _____

   _____

3. _____

   _____

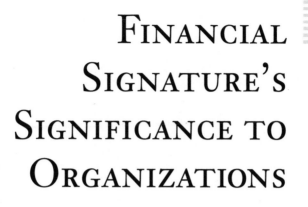

FINANCIAL SIGNATURE'S SIGNIFICANCE TO ORGANIZATIONS

THE FINANCIAL MISSION'S EFFECT ON AN ORGANIZATION

Even in the short term, the financial signature of a leader will improve or weaken the three basic functions within any company—sales, products or services, and operations. In this chapter, we will use the four extremes of the nine financial missions, namely the Buccaneer (High/Low), the Mercantilist (Low/High), the Venture Capitalist (High/High), and the Discounter (Low/Low), to assess the effect of each financial mission on these three areas.

Financial Mission and Sales Performance

A leader's financial signature has a direct and visible effect on her company's sales performance. On the one hand, a leader with a high propensity for value adding, other things being equal, will have a positive effect on sales growth by virtue of increased customer demand. On the other hand, a leader's low level of resource utilization will also affect investments in sales and marketing.

Buccaneers generally have high sales growth. Although relatively low resource utilization normally leads to low sales growth, the Buccaneer uses a high level of value adding to put her company in a strong competitive position. A well-differentiated product or service with few substitutes leads to high customer demand and corresponding high sales growth.

Sandy Weill is a good example of a Buccaneer. Throughout his career, each company he added to his portfolio increased sales rapidly. At Smith Barney, for example, he increased margins by focusing his brokers on maximizing the amount of margin debt their customers took on. Allowing customers to use their portfolios as collateral—not just for stocks but also for consumer items—increased their use of their Smith Barney accounts. The resulting higher retail sales for his brokers led to commission increases too, from the industry average of $270,000 up to $500,000.[1]

Weill also achieved rapid sales growth by bottom-fishing—picking up brokerage enterprises when they were in trouble. He acquired part of Drexel Burnham's troubled business from Gerald Tsai for a paltry $4 million after its leader, Michael Milliken, was sent to jail. He thus increased annual revenues by $100 million and annual profits by $20 million.

The Mercantilist is the polar opposite of the Buccaneer, having a tendency toward low value adding and high resource utilization. On the face of it, high resource utilization should lead to a higher investment in sales and marketing and, consequently, high sales growth. Value adding is low, however, which leads to low competitiveness and low demand because the customer perceives little value in the company's products and services. This situation frequently occurs in mature industries, where high advertising and sales expenses leave the company stymied, and no amount of sales or advertising will persuade customers to expand their purchases.

An example of a Mercantilist is Chuck Conaway, the CEO of Kmart in the late 1990s who preceded its bankruptcy filing. Conaway had a low level of value-adding propensity and a high level of resource utilization. He was probably the last person Kmart should have recruited as its leader. His high-spending ways as CEO were legendary, complete with excessive executive compensation, personal extravagances, and frequent use of the corporate jet for personal travel.

Under Conaway, Kmart's hallmark, the BlueLight Special, was reintroduced. It had never been effective, however, and, not surprisingly, it failed the second time around as well. In the aftermath of Conaway's tenure, Kmart entered bankruptcy, a frequent result of a Mercantilist leader.

Like the Buccaneer, the Venture Capitalist also drives high sales growth with products or services that have a high level of value added. The main difference between the two is that the Venture Capitalist has high resource utilization, strengthening sales growth through major investments in marketing, while the Buccaneer has self-sustaining demand even with relatively low resource utilization. As long as the Venture Capitalist funds sales and marketing at a high level, demand and sales growth will follow. The Buccaneer, on the other hand, doesn't need to utilize this high level of resources to generate sales.

Steve Jobs of Apple is an example of the Venture Capitalist financial signature. Apple's sales growth was very high for many years, driven by the very high–value-added Macintosh computer and its proprietary operating system. Customers were drawn to the early model Apple computer not by high-pressure sales but by its compelling value—an easy-to-use, affordable computer.

Today, just as twenty years ago, Apple's sales growth is being driven by a high–value-added product—the iPod. The iPod does not need to be sold, it is a must-have item for many of the digerati. This time around, however, Jobs's conversion to a Profiteer financial mission is providing better margins than during his first stint as CEO. Jobs reflects the potential in many leaders to improve their leadership outcomes by consciously changing their financial missions.

The Discounter is the polar opposite of the Venture Capitalist. With the Discounter, there is little or no hope for any sales growth, nor value added to spur customer demand, nor resources available to compensate for low value adding. The result is a zero-sum game among the players, often in a mature industry, where no company is experiencing sales growth. Only another player with higher value added can break out of this vicious cycle.

An excellent example of a Discounter is Reginald Lewis, whose leveraged buyout (LBO) of Beatrice was one of the largest deals of this type ever, following his equally successful LBO of McCall. The hallmark of Lewis's style was that he was a hands-off owner who added no value to the companies he acquired. Instead, he was a financial engineer, acquiring enterprises in the classic LBO style. He had no vision for the companies except to make money, which he did well.

Lewis's style of low resource utilization led to stagnant or declining sales growth at the companies he bought, but he still came out ahead financially. In the case of McCall, he later sold it for a profit. In the case of Beatrice, he sold off the nonperforming parts of the enterprise but held on to the moneymaking assets.

Financial Mission and Product Performance

Each of the four financial mission archetypes—Buccaneer, Mercantilist, Venture Capitalist, and Discounter—has a characteristic effect on three corporate product competencies: competitiveness, quality, and customer satisfaction.

Behind the Buccaneer's success are very competitive, highly differentiated, and new or novel products and services. These products and services put the competition on the defensive and result in major barriers to entry. In the Buccaneer's enterprise category, his product or service is the only such player or the only feasible player.

In the area of product quality, however, things are not so rosy. The high growth rate of the Buccaneer's enterprise frequently results in product and service snags and poor customer support. And as growth climbs, quality worsens. The Buccaneer's predilection for high growth rarely allows him to slow down and correct product quality issues. The Buccaneer's focus is on making money, at the expense of anything and everything else.

This leads to major problems in the area of customer satisfaction. The Buccaneer's company being the only game in town frequently leads to arrogance on the part of the company and its CEO. But because the customer has nowhere else to go, the company has little incentive to divert resources to improve customer satisfaction. The Buccaneer's focus on performance can lead to customers who dislike the company even though they cannot do without it.

One of the best-known Buccaneers is Bill Gates of Microsoft. He and his company have repeatedly chosen earnings over customer support and product quality, as evidenced by its recent massive dividend distributions. Meanwhile, customer satisfaction continues to be a challenge for the company, where its software still has product quality issues.

Despite grousing about software bugs, customers have continued to buy Microsoft products. There is no comparable alternative that meets their needs better, so they stick with what works. Gates's propensity for high value adding has produced highly competitive products, but the lack of urgency about fixing software glitches still irritates even the most loyal customers.

The Mercantilist has products and service that are considered commodities. Many competitors in the marketplace all offer exactly the same type of product or service with little or no differentiation. This is a tough place to be.

But in the area of quality, the Mercantilist usually shines. Because the company's product or service is usually in a mature market, the Mercantilist's high level of resource utilization facilitates investment in quality, even when it is not cost-effective. The company culture is so invested in its product and the customer experience that it will continue to invest in quality initiatives even when it does not make financial sense. This makes for strong customer satisfaction. High resource utilization leads to significant expenses and investment in the area of customer support.

Often the Mercantilist runs a company that has a well-established brand name, yet it continues to invest in brand-building activities—a by-product of the leader's high resource utilization. Robert Allen, the erstwhile chairman of AT&T, is an excellent example of a Mercantilist.

In assessing the declining profitability of the Mercantilist, mainly due to high resource utilization, enterprises recruiting a new leader may want to ask themselves whether they want high profits or high quality—having both may not be an option long-term. For many stockholders, if not their boards, the answer is obvious: Go with the Buccaneer, who has found a way to increase sales growth even with questionable quality.

The Venture Capitalist's products typically are high value adding and well differentiated. However, because the products and services are often new introductions, frequently quality issues and other problems arise that need to be worked out. And with new products, it is difficult to predict where quality problems will come up and what the effect on customer satisfaction will be. The Venture Capitalist has a high level of resource utilization but directs funds more toward product innovation than toward quality.

All this leads to customer satisfaction weakness. With low quality comes many product returns and a good deal of customer dissatisfaction. The vast majority of customers are not pioneers or early adopters and will not accept the product's many flaws. The Venture Capitalist leader's tendency to innovate to the detriment of supporting existing products and services only adds to customer dissatisfaction.

One of the quintessential examples of the Venture Capitalist financial mission is Larry Ellison of Oracle. Ellison's propensity to add value led to his development of an entirely new class of software—databases.

This new product led to very high sales growth. Ellison's tendencies toward high resource utilization also led to major investments in sales and marketing, which reinforced the company's sales growth. But his focus on sales growth also led to major quality problems.

In the early 1990s, Oracle's quality problems became so acute that it nearly went bankrupt. Even today, Oracle continues to struggle with customer satisfaction, though its recent problems stem more from pricing-related issues than from product quality. This shift also reflects Ellison's shift from the Venture Capitalist mission to Buccaneer, which is his financial mission now.

In the area of competitiveness, however, the Venture Capitalist leads the way. Ellison's focus on value adding led to Oracle's major competitive advantage and crowded out all the early competitors.

Not surprising, the Discounter ranks low in the area of competitiveness because this style has low value adding and low resource utilization. The product is undifferentiated, often in a pure commodity market, and the only way to succeed is by keeping costs to an absolute minimum.

What may be a surprise is the typically high quality of the Discounter's product. Because this product is usually in a mature product category, where customer needs and responses are well understood and where an immense amount of experience in manufacturing and delivery has been accumulated, it takes very little to keep quality at a high level.

Customer satisfaction with the Discounter is often high, too. The product is undifferentiated, so it looks exactly like everyone else's and customers do not expect much support. Because the product is mature, it generally reflects the product features customers have historically demonstrated they want. The low price of the product boosts customer satisfaction as well. Any qualms the customer has about the quality of the product or services are more than offset by its very low price.

An inverse relationship exists between competitiveness and product quality/customer satisfaction for the four financial missions. High competitiveness is associated with low quality and customer satisfaction, while low competitiveness is correlated with high quality and customer satisfaction. Only rarely do the two correspond. Companies such as Toyota, which is highly competitive while maintaining high quality and customer satisfaction, are the exception, not the rule.

Where the leader's financial signature focuses on value added, quality and customer issues are neglected. Where the leader is low in value-adding propensity, she compensates by increasing the emphasis on quality and customer satisfaction. Unfortunately for the low value-adding mission, however, this does not usually lead to the desired high-profit outcome.

Financial Mission and Operations Performance

Buccaneers, Mercantilists, Venture Capitalists, and Discounters can also be distinguished by their characteristic level of execution—their ability to develop, deliver, and maintain the company's products while simultaneously ensuring the company's financial viability. There are significant differences between the four financial missions on this point.

With respect to execution, the Buccaneer fares very well. Although quality issues arise, the Buccaneer's very low resource utilization levels actually increase her execution capability. The Buccaneer's strong determination to keep expenses low results in a high level of creativity to develop efficient processes that reduce execution costs.

The success of Michael Dell of Dell Computers shows that low costs are not, as one would expect, associated with low levels of execution. Dell is very low in the area of resource utilization. According to Kevin Rollins, its president, "There are some organizations where people think they're a hero if they invent a new thing. . . . Being a hero at Dell means saving money."[2]

Yet Dell has defined the very essence of execution. Its system of delivering totally customized PCs to consumers has revolutionized the business of selling them. Low resource utilization led to huge levels of creativity at Dell, which led to a breakthrough in processes to execute its business mission.

The Mercantilist, in contrast to the Buccaneer, is poor in execution. After many years of experience in a mature market with the same products and customers, the Mercantilist resists change. Instead of improving execution, the Mercantilist's years of experience actually hamper his ability to become more efficient. High levels of resource utilization also perpetuate inefficient ways of doing things. Ultimately, the Mercantilist's financial signature leads to poor and ever-deteriorating performance in execution.

Occasionally, a leader will see the problems inherent in a Mercantilist financial mission and take corrective action. Roberto Goizueta, the former CEO of Coca-Cola, is a case in point.

Before Goizueta, Coca-Cola, a Mercantilist-style company, did its own bottling. Goizueta saw that the high fixed costs of bottling were strangling the company. He developed and executed a new plan to sell off the bottling to independent businesses. This allowed Coca-Cola to focus on manufacturing its proprietary syrup, and marketing. At the same time, selling off its bottling operations allowed the company to reduce its debt and increase its margins, thereby increasing its own ability to execute.

Goizueta was not a Mercantilist, he was actually a Consolidator—medium value adding and medium resource utilization. He moved Coca-Cola away from its excessive dependence on the Mercantilist financial mission and, in doing so, actually led to a resurgence in Coca-Cola's sales and margins.

But this resurgence lasted only as long as Goizueta did. When he left, the company reverted to its Mercantilist mission and recruited or promoted leaders with similar financial missions. As a result, the company's sales and execution levels have declined and it is now back in the same position it was before Goizueta took the helm.

The Venture Capitalist is also low in the area of execution—but for the opposite reasons of the Mercantilist. In the case of the Venture Capitalist, the leader is far more interested in issues of innovation and market acceptance than in execution.

The Venture Capitalist's propensity toward high value adding, unlike that of the Buccaneer's, does not pass over into the area of execution, even though it might appear that it would be highly advantageous to do so. His high resource utilization is also directed primarily at product innovation rather than execution. Steve Jobs was legendary at Apple and NEXT Computer for producing innovative products, but also for failing to deliver enough products on time.

In contrast, the Discounter is strong on the execution front. His low resource utilization and low value adding prove to be an incentive, spurring creativity in execution just as it does for the Buccaneer. In both cases, the determination to keep costs low results in a high level of creativity in finding new ways to execute.

Both the Discounter and the Buccaneer move mountains to find new ways to execute in low-cost ways. The Buccaneer does it to increase earnings even further, while the Discounter does it to stave off imminent bankruptcy. In both cases, the result is the same, namely, an increased capability to execute. The lack of financial resources or their deliberate constraint can prove an effective means of encouraging creativity in matters corporate.

Career Choices and Financial Mission

Your financial signature will have a characteristic effect on the short-term performance of your organization. It will affect your organization's sales, products, and operations in ways that you need to be aware of. Where the effect of your financial mission is not what your organization needs, you may need to make a concerted effort to change.

You can decide whether your financial style reflects the effect you want to have on your enterprise. If not, you can develop a plan to change the outcome for the better, to help your company and your career.

Notes

1 M. Langley, *Tearing Down the Walls: How Sandy Weill Fought His Way to the Top of the Financial World . . . and Then Nearly Lost It All*, New York: Simon and Schuster, 2003, 181.

2 A. Park and P. Burrows, "What You Don't Know About Dell," *Business Week*, November 3, 2003, 79.

How Financial Signature Affects an Enterprise

This chapter demonstrated that:

▶ A leader's financial mission affects the sales growth of a company through the value-added driver— higher value added leads to increased customer demand and, thus, sales.

▶ A leader's financial mission has characteristic effects on the products and services of a company: on its competitiveness, product quality, and customer satisfaction.

▶ A leader's financial mission has characteristic effects on the leader's capability to execute—lower levels of resource utilization can actually drive higher levels of execution, while established enterprises in mature industries with high levels of resource utilization have a reduced ability to execute.

Top Two Takeaways

▶ Your financial mission will affect your sales, products, and operations in characteristic ways.

▶ Restricting available resources will result in better, not worse, execution.

SELF-DEVELOPMENT EXERCISE

Assess how your financial mission has affected your organization's sales, products, and operations over the past twelve months.

Sales

_____

_____

_____

_____

Products

_____

_____

_____

_____

Operations

_____

_____

_____

_____

ALIGNING FINANCIAL MISSION WITH AN ORGANIZATION

The culture of an organization reflects one of the nine financial missions. Whether or not the company's leader has created that culture, these nine missions define all of the feasible business cultures for any organization. These cultures can thus be named according to the missions, hence the Buccaneer culture, the Mercantilist culture, and so on.

A leader may have been selected to fit in with an existing business culture or to change it; either way, he becomes a part of it. In some cases, a new leader takes over an organization and does change its culture. By referring to the leader's financial mission, we can see where the organizational culture started and where it is headed. More important, it will show us the pattern of financial performance and profitability associated with the culture and how this pattern may change as a result of the leadership change.

In some cases, a new leader's financial mission does not match the culture of the organization, which poses a problem. The financial mission of the leader, whether a

CEO or a new manager, needs to be aligned with the culture of the organization. If it is not, there will be conflicts over how to achieve ongoing positive financial performance. Unless resolved, this disparity alone will likely lead to the organization's downfall, in both profit and operational performance.

Matched Financial Missions

Lou Gerstner, the Matched Conglomerator

An example of what happens when a leader and his organization have the same mission involves Lou Gerstner's tenture at IBM. Gerstner's Conglomerator financial mission comprised a medium value adding and a high propensity for resource utilization. In other words, he had a Deficit financial style.

IBM also had a Conglomerator culture. Its value adding had declined to a medium level as it lost its innovative touch and became a mature organization. Its level of resource utilization was also high. From that viewpoint, the two were well matched.

At IBM, Gerstner was a brilliant turnaround manager, but his lack of value-adding perspective is demonstrated in the loss of the personal computer (PC) market share under his tenure.[1] As a Conglomerator, Gerstner's instinctive approach to growing the company was by acquisition. The Lotus acquisition occurred precisely for this reason.[2] Gerstner implicitly conceded through his own decisions that his financial signature was not going to result in growing IBM internally.

Gross margins declined under Gerstner as he shifted from high–value-added, proprietary hardware to lower gross margin services. These services put IBM at the bottom of the value-adding rankings in the technology industry although, overall, still in the medium value-adding category.

On the other hand, Gerstner was a high-expense CEO. With a background at McKinsey and several large enterprises, he could not have been otherwise. His massive $25 billion buyback of IBM stock in 1997 reflected an approach that was based on a very high level of resource utilization—his staff cutbacks in IBM notwithstanding. Only expensive acquisitions, notably Lotus, allowed him to grow IBM so that it could keep up, both technologically and financially.

Gerstner was exactly what IBM needed at that particular stage of its company evolution—someone who did not have a high level of value adding. IBM had essentially run out of new products—its mainframes—and was under attack from the new PC market. It had lost its technological edge in the market and was seen as a laggard.

And although Gerstner was high on the resource utilization scale, that too was what IBM needed at that particular juncture. The company had the resources, and Gerstner was prepared to use them to conduct one of the largest stock buybacks ever.

Gerstner was successful because IBM's Conglomerator culture and Gerstner's own Conglomerator financial signature fit together perfectly. At this particular stage of the company's evolution, it needed a Conglomerator.

Gerstner's case demonstrates that a leader can have a Deficit style and still succeed. In this case, however, the positive effect is short-term. A Deficit type, or indeed a Gerstner, would not be a good fit as a longer-term leader. A Deficit leader is useful for helping a company through a transition but is not a good long-term choice as a leader because of the losses in market value—if not profitability—that accompany such leadership styles over time.

While Lou Gerstner was the perfect choice for IBM, John Sculley's Venture Capitalist financial style was a bad fit at Apple.

Mismatched Financial Missions

John Sculley, the Mismatched Venture Capitalist

At PepsiCo, John Sculley was the highly successful vice president of marketing. His record there indicates that he had a low level of value adding and a propensity for high resource utilization—a Mercantilist. Thus, Sculley had a Deficit financial style.

Coming from PepsiCo, a low-innovation company, where he had served for many years, to Apple, a high-innovation company, Sculley knew that he had to reinvent himself. Apple also had a Venture Capitalist culture, so he remade himself into a Venture Capitalist. He became a visionary. In so doing, Sculley emulated his visionary boss,

Steve Jobs. The problem was that he needed to be different from Jobs, not the same, and he unfortunately didn't realize that.

As competitive threats mounted, Apple needed a different type of financial mission and a different kind of leader. The time for a Venture Capitalist had passed, and Sculley was never going to be better for Apple than Jobs. Apple needed a Buccaneer or a Profiteer, and Sculley was neither.

Sculley failed in his transition to a Venture Capitalist financial mission. His Mercantilist instincts took the company down-market with a lack of value added. The board recognized this and ultimately forced him to resign.

Matched and Mismatched Financial Missions

Al Dunlap, the Deceived Discounter

Al Dunlap of Sunbeam infamy was a Discounter—low value adding and low resource utilization.

Sunbeam had a Trader culture—low value adding and medium resource utilization. The company needed a leader with a medium value-adding propensity and medium level of resource utilization—a Consolidator. A Profiteer, with medium resource utilization and high value adding, would also have worked. What Sunbeam got, however, was a Discounter, someone used to dressing up companies for a profitable sale. The result was dissatisfaction all around.

Dunlap's investor backers really wanted someone with a Buccaneer financial signature. They wanted fast growth in the short term. But Dunlap's irrepressible urge to cut savagely would not make such growth possible. And the high–value-adding nature of a Buccaneer would have been inconsistent with Sunbeam's low value-adding culture.

The board and private investors in Sunbeam were sophisticated market players and investors, yet they still failed to make a good choice in Dunlap. Despite their knowledge, they failed to understand the need for congruent financial missions between the organization and the leader.

How Market Evolution Affects Financial Mission Requirements

The financial signature requirements of an organization differ depending on the stage of the market in which it operates.

If the market is early stage, for example, the enterprise needs a high level of value adding to succeed and, to achieve earnings early on, a low level of resource utilization—in other words, it needs a Buccaneer. Frequently, however, this type of organization will recruit a leader who has a Venture Capitalist or Consolidator financial mission, the latter frequently possessed by someone from an established company in a mature industry. Or it may hire a leader with a Mercantilist financial signature. This often happens in early-stage enterprises backed by Venture Capitalists who decide that they need a very experienced executive and recruit a leader who has spent most of her working life in a large company. All too often, this strategy will result in failure for the organization—and the investors.

As the market consolidates, organizational requirements shift. With competitors appearing, the company needs a high or medium level of value adding and a medium to low level of resource utilization—a Profiteer or an Arbitrageur. Unfortunately, the organization usually hires a leader with a Conglomerator or Trader financial signature, resulting in poor financial performance.

Finally, as the market matures, an enterprise requires a leader with a medium level of value adding and a low level of resource utilization—an Arbitrageur. Again, the organization often hires a leader with a Trader or Discounter financial signature, which leads to poor or failing outcomes.

As an example of this scenario, let's take a look at George Shaheen, the able but controversial leader of an outstanding firm, Andersen Consulting. Shaheen was instrumental in precipitating the breakup of Arthur Andersen into two enterprises, but he left in 1999 to become the CEO of Webvan, the start-up online grocery company. Less than two years later, Shaheen resigned, and Webvan later went into liquidation.

Shaheen was an example of an Old Economy leader who went into a New Economy company. As the erstwhile leader of a major company, his background, experience, and comfort levels were with enterprises that operated in mature industries. His financial signature was a medium level of value adding, and he had a medium level of resource utilization—a classic Consolidator financial mission.

But this was not the financial mission that Webvan required. It needed a Buccaneer or, at worst, a Venture Capitalist. Shaheen was neither, and his financial signature was clearly unsuited to Webvan. Of course, Webvan hired Shaheen for his name and contacts, not his financial style, and it paid the ultimate price.

The dot-com era saw several similar cases, such as Joseph Galli of Black & Decker, who moved to Amazon; Heidi Miller, the former CFO of Citigroup, who left for Priceline; and Bill Maloy of AT&T, who went to Peapod. All three later left these enterprises under similar circumstances to Shaheen's departure from Webvan. These Old Economy leaders tended to have the same Consolidator financial mission, a bad fit for the New Economy start-ups that required a Buccaneer or Profiteer financial mission.

The selection committee of an enterprise often has a hard time deciding on any leader, let alone a leader whose selection would be dependent on the stage of market evolution. Furthermore, getting a consensus on what the company's stage of evolution is can also be difficult. But if the organization does not make either of these decisions, it risks hiring a leader whose financial signature is simply going to harm it through lack of alignment and an inappropriate financial style.

How Product Evolution Affects Financial Mission Requirements

Just as with a company, a product requires leaders with different financial signatures and missions as it matures.

In the early stages of product development, an organization requires a leader with a high propensity for value adding. While expenses need to be relatively high to undertake this development, it cannot be so high as to imperil company survival. Yet, all too often, the company hires a leader with a Venture Capitalist financial mission—with potentially adverse consequences.

Once the product is developed, the organization's needs change. The company now requires a leader who focuses less on value adding and more on reducing expenses—an Arbitrageur financial mission. Yet it often gets one with a Trader or Conglomerator financial mission, which leads to major problems.

As the product reaches maturity, the enterprise needs a leader with an Arbitrageur financial style. All too often, at this stage, its board recruits a leader with a Discounter financial mission, believing that this is the only way it can get out of the box it finds itself in.

How financial signature interacts with product evolution is not always quite as simple in real life as it is on paper. Let's take Case 7, the CEO of an early-stage technology company.

Case 7 had started a company based on technology he had licensed from another venture. The good news was that his start-up expenses were not very high, as he had not had to develop the technology himself. He merely had to refine and extend it to the particular application he had in mind.

Case 7 was an Arbitrageur—medium value adding and low resource utilization. As such, his financial mission was intrinsically profitable. Consequently, his company evaded the large losses that typically characterize an early-stage company with an early-stage product. The money he raised was more than enough to keep the company going.

But the company never made large inroads into the market. Its product had a place, but its level of value added was not enough to make it attractive to many buyers. Competitors crept in with similar offerings licensed from the same company that had developed the technology in the first place. And Case 7's intrinsically profitable financial mission was simply not providing enough value to result in a very attractive product.

Contrast Case 7 with Case 8, the CEO of another technology company. Case 8 started his company and developed his product from scratch. But Case 8 was a Buccaneer—high value adding and low resource utilization. Although it was a difficult task, he found a way to make profits even though his product was at an early stage.

Case 8 acquired another company that was public and put the product into the existing vehicle. He quickly made profits. He had a propensity for very low resource utilization, which led to low expenses in his company. Against all of the odds, he made money with a start-up product. The Buccaneer financial mission worked in his favor.

Case 7 and Case 8 show us that early-stage enterprises can be viable and even successful as long as they have a leader with the correct and intrinsically profitable financial mission. Case 7's company was viable but not attractive. As an Arbitrageur, he simply did not deliver enough value to thrive, although he delivered enough to survive. Case 8, though, was different. His Buccaneer financial mission led to the potentially outsized earnings that characterize this financial mission, even though his product was at an early stage.

In most cases, unfortunately, enterprises hire leaders with financial signatures and missions that lead to early failure or, at best, poor performance. Most organizations chalk this up to the intrinsic difficulties of starting or growing a new enterprise or getting a new product to market. They are partially right.

Few realize, however, that there is another way: recruit a leader with a Surplus financial style. The process may still be tough, but this sort of leader will dramatically increase the odds of survival and success.

Enterprise Evolution and Financial Mission

As an enterprise undergoes its standard life cycle, it needs leaders with different types of financial missions. Mostly, it will need Surplus styles. On occasion, it could also use leaders with a Deficit style to meet particular internal or external circumstances—but only for relatively short periods.

Because there are only three Surplus styles, there are few choices. At the early stages of an enterprise, a Buccaneer is clearly the best choice. As the enterprise hits its stride, more issues will surface, usually making the Profiteer a smart choice. At the later stages, the Arbitrageur is the best option for most enterprises, as she is able to wring out every last ounce of value even when the going is tough.

The required financial missions are set out in Figure 6.1. To be successful, the financial mission needs to be above the line. But in particular circumstances, the financial missions below the line could also be useful to the enterprise—provided that it realizes the limitations of such leaders. When an enterprise does not understand how enterprise evolution intersects with financial mission, it will often hire leaders with Deficit styles at the points we have indicated in the diagram.

As a company evolves, it makes typical mistakes in selecting its leaders. In the earlier stage of growth or at rebirth, it tends to recruit leaders with a Venture Capitalist financial mission. In the short term, this may be a good decision, just to get things going. But if it sticks with such a leader, it will experience problems of enterprise sustainability.

Jean Marie Messier of Vivendi had a Venture Capitalist financial signature, one unsuited to an ex-utility. Vivendi should have quickly fired Messier and put in a

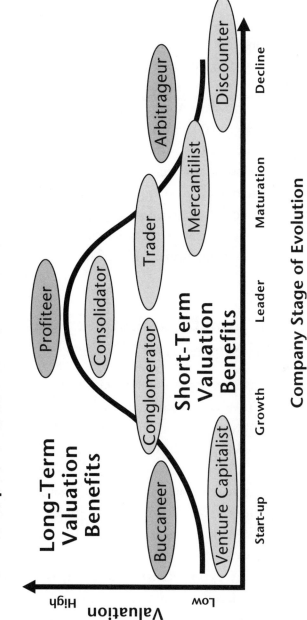

FIGURE 6.1 Enterprise evolution and financial mission.

Buccaneer or Profiteer. Gerald Levin of Time Warner also had a Venture Capitalist financial signature—hence, the disastrous merger with America Online. Time Warner should have recruited a Buccaneer or Profiteer.

As a company progresses through the various stages of evolution, similar choices emerge. An enterprise will often shy away from the three good choices and move to the likely failing ones. These range from the Venture Capitalist, Consolidator, and Discounter, who at least have a minimal chance of success over the longer term, to the even worse ones of Trader, Conglomerator, and Mercantilist, who basically have no chance of success in the long term, at least without some form of intervention.

Organizational Conflict with the Financial Signature

In the long term, an organization should only recruit leaders who possess a Surplus financial style—the Buccaneer, the Profiteer, and the Arbitrageur. A leader with any other financial style is simply going to do it no good—and probably a lot of harm—over the long term. While a leader may appear to be great in many ways, unless the recruiting organization can be absolutely sure of the leader's profit-making potential, it should first assess his financial signature.

The one exception is that a board may recruit a leader with a Deficit financial mission to achieve certain short-term purposes. But the enterprise needs to know exactly what it is doing to avoid potential short-term losses, not to mention a declining long-term financial performance.

Making and sustaining profits in an unforgiving and competitive marketplace is difficult. The theory of financial signature adds another set of constraints. If a leader has a Deficit style, he faces an additional hurdle—fighting the very persona and internal drives that propelled him into a leadership position in the first place. How easy is it for anyone to fight what made him successful?

There is a way out of this dilemma. The enterprise needs to support the leader in ways that will help him transition to a financial mission with a better chance for success. We will discuss how to do this in Chapter 9.

Alignment of Culture and Financial Mission

For emerging leaders and those in midlevel positions, this chapter has a number of important consequences:

- Alignment between a leader's personal financial mission and the culture of the organization is critical. If it does not exist, the leader is likely to have a tough time, no matter how talented she is.
- Success in an organization over the long term is also dependent on the leader's having a Surplus style.
- If a leader does not have a Surplus style, he should learn how to acquire one.

- A leader with a Deficit style in an organization with a Deficit culture, or a leader with a Puzzler style in a Puzzler culture, despite their aligned styles, will not achieve much. The organization will likely fail or underperform because of the combination of financial style and culture.

In sum, alignment of missions may be key, but the culture also has to be correct.

Notes

1 D. Garr, *IBM Redux: Lou Gerstner and the Business Turnaround of the Decade*, New York: HarperCollins, 1999, 305.

2 Ibid., 218.

Aligning Financial Mission with the Organization

This chapter demonstrated that:

▶ For a leader to succeed, his or her financial signature must be congruent with the organization's culture.

▶ In addition, the organization's culture must have a Surplus financial mission for the long term.

▶ When an organization recruits a leader with a Deficit style, its goals are usually fundamentally in conflict with those of the leader.

▶ Leaders with Deficit financial missions can produce positive financial performances, but only in the short term.

▶ A leader's financial signature must be congruent with the organization's level of market, product, and enterprise evolution.

Top Two Takeaways

▶ Check the culture of any organization that you intend to join to make sure that it aligns with your financial signature.

▶ In addition, check that the culture of the organization is a Surplus style.

SELF-DEVELOPMENT EXERCISE

Complete the Financial Signature Self-Assessment in the
Appendix. This will provide you with an objective assessment
of the alignment between your financial mission and the
culture of your organization.

CHAPTER 7

How a Financial Mission Evolves

Some leaders are average. Some perform very well. What causes the difference? And how do leaders' financial missions evolve to match their organization's financial needs?

Early in their career, leaders are in an intense learning stage. They know little about leadership, make frequent mistakes, and are, in effect, apprentice leaders. As leaders develop and grow, however, they become competent practitioners. While they may not be expert yet, they have picked up the basic elements of leadership.

Business leaders may be deemed experienced if they have had more than five years of experience. However, only a small percentage of the apprentice and practitioner leaders will survive to the experienced stage.

Once they have moved through the experienced stage, leaders can become expert, or what we call master leaders. At that stage they are, indeed, masters of their craft. They have learned enough that they may survive at that level indefinitely. Master leaders, needless to say, are not common.

What drives leaders to these rarified levels? In the case of Surplus types, they have maximized the potential of their financial mission. In the case of Deficit types, they have compensated for it.

The evolution of leaders, in fact, is the evolution of their financial mission. If they are lucky enough to have a Surplus financial signature, they are already on their way to being successful. But if, like most leaders, they do not yet have a Surplus style, they need to compensate somehow. The difference between average and successful leaders is how well they compensate for a financially underperforming style.

Correction Process of Financial Mission

The correction process of the financial mission is the process by which a leader learns to compensate for her financial signature. The uncorrected stage of this process is the time during which a leader has not yet compensated for her financial mission. This stage leads to an *uncorrected outcome* for the company, which is failing financial performance.

Once a leader has learned to compensate for her financial mission, she has reached the corrected stage and the company's resulting financial performance is the *corrected outcome*. Reaching this stage also signals a leader's achieving master leader status. If a leader wants any chance to succeed, she will have to correct.

During the uncorrected stage, a leader emphasizes and reinforces her natural financial signature. After all, those strengths made her a leader. If a leader has a Surplus style, for example, she will reinforce it, leading to even better financial performance for her company. But if she is a Deficit leader, she will continue to reinforce that style, achieving financial underperformance and possibly ending up being fired.

By the corrected stage, the master leader has learned to identify, strengthen, and reinforce compensating and balancing behavior, to counteract potentially failing financial tendencies. During this stage, if the business leader has a Surplus financial mission, she will strengthen it. If she has a Deficit financial mission, she will have learned how to compensate for it.

Patterns in Financial Mission Correction

How often do CEOs recognize a need to compensate for their failing behavior? Using direct observation and interviews, we have identified patterns with respect to their corrected and uncorrected behavior.

First, prior experience made a difference for the leaders in our study. First-time business leaders were equally divided between corrected and uncorrected behavior. But in the group of leaders who had previously held senior executive positions, twice as many were corrected as uncorrected.

What about founders? Conventional wisdom suggests that founders are more headstrong and independent than nonfounding business leaders and thus would be less likely to correct their behavior. But that is not borne out by our research, which shows that both founders and nonfounders experienced a similar rate of correction.

Two factors had a significant effect on business leaders' propensity to correct. The first was age. In our sample of business leaders, those under fifty years old were more likely to have uncorrected behavior, while those over fifty were very likely to have corrected their behavior.

The second factor was whether business leaders were in a partnership. Those who were not in a partnership were as likely to be uncorrected as not. Business leaders in a partnership, however, were twice as likely to be corrected. Partnerships clearly confer a huge advantage on their participants. But there are different types of partnerships and different levels of their effect.

Ultimately, whether leaders had a Surplus or Deficit financial signature is not the main issue; whether they have learned to correct for their financial mission is. Leaders who do not correct their financial mission have not learned how to compensate for their financial signature. The self-awareness that allows correction is the main difference between successful and failing leaders.

Principles of Correction

How do leaders correct their financial mission? Although Surplus style leaders are, technically, already corrected, there are a variety of patterns of evolution among Deficit, Puzzler, and even Surplus leaders.

Remember that a leader does not change his financial signature, he simply modifies his behavior. For successful leaders who have corrected, it may often appear that they have funadmentally changed. When under significant stress, however, they will occasionally revert to type, going back to their natural financial style.

Leaders may change, or correct, in the desired direction, but there are limits to how much they can change. No leader feels comfortable with behavior that departs radically from his natural financial signature. For example, we cannot expect leaders with low value-adding tendencies to suddenly feel comfortable in high value-adding situations. Nor will leaders with a propensity for high resource utilization feel comfortable with very low resource utilization. This is simply not realistic. Movement in a particular direction is possible, however.

In terms of value-adding behavior, most leaders find it difficult, but not impossible, to move strongly up the value-adding scale. But even with such movement, they likely travel just one level up, say, from low to medium or from medium to high. They simply do not recognize strategies that create higher value added. As for resource utilization, most leaders find it difficult to move down more than one level, and even that may stretch them psychologically. They are simply not attuned to thinking at that level about these issues.

This limited movement has an important implication, as it limits the types of transitions that leaders can make between financial missions. Although the diagrams may make it appear as if leaders can move anywhere, this is not the case.

Five Financial Mission Bands

We can now view the financial missions from a different perspective. All of the financial missions lead to different levels of profitability, yet some financial performance patterns (grouped into shaded bands in Figure 7.1) are similarly sustainable long term. That is, some financial performance patterns have the same profit quality, even if they represent different financial missions.

In Figure 7.1, the nine financial missions are categorized into five profit-quality bands, with those in Band 1 being the most desirable. Those missions in the same band exhibit the same profit quality, despite their differences in profitability.

The profit-quality bands show us what a leader can and can't achieve by transitioning between financial missions as well as whether any progress has been made. Even if he seems to have made an appropriately good move, say, from Trader to Conglomerator, this diagram shows he has not achieved anything, because he has traded higher value adding for higher resource utilization. Other things being equal, the leader is no better off. Although he has transitioned between styles, they are still both failing styles in the same profit-quality band.

Transitions within bands may look good, but they generally achieve nothing for the company. The profit-

FIGURE 7.1 The five profit-quality bands.

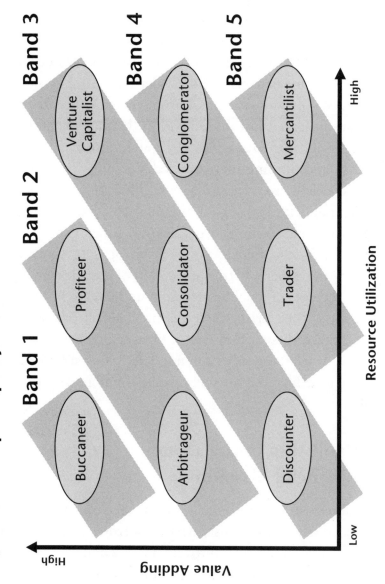

quality bands make it clear that true progression is from the lower right to the higher left bands.

Leaders frequently make transitions between styles in the same financial band. Under Kenneth Lay and Jeffrey Skilling, for example, Enron seemed to become a star. But, in fact, it just moved within the same band, from a Consolidator to a Venture Capitalist financial mission. Lay and Skilling increased value adding at the cost of increasing resource utilization. This strategy was great for publicity but not for the shareholders. Enron was a zero-sum transition, also known as a shell game.

Leaders often make such changes to spark some action—either a better perception of their leadership or, in the case of a public company, an increase in the company's stock price. In terms of financial performance, however, these actions are of little lasting benefit.

With these caveats in mind, let's look at how each of the nine financial missions evolves in more detail.

Evolution of the Deficit Financial Missions

Mercantilists have limits on what they can transition to. Normally, Mercantilists transition from Band 5 to Band 4, which is a real improvement, becoming Traders or Conglomerators. But transitioning to Puzzlers in Band 3 is beyond most Mercantilists. Although Traders and Conglomerators are still in Deficit territory, they are better than the alternatives and still offer better profitability outcomes than Mercantilists.

Mercantilists are a rare breed. They exist but then go out of business so quickly that they are often not around long enough to study. Of the CEOs we studied, almost all of the Mercantilists were uncorrected.

One example of a Mercentilist masquerading as a Discounter is Donald Burr of People's Express, a famous low-fare airline from the 1980s. Burr had been in the airline business for many years, as part of Continental, before starting People's Express. Burr had learned the trade at the feet of a financial, not an operating, master in Frank Lorenzo. His concept for People's Express called for adding no value of his own other than the idea of cutting costs to the bone, just as Continental had tried. He was a low value-adding leader.

Burr also had high resource utilization. Being part of the airline business automatically made him a member of this club, because airlines are a very high-expense business. They have enormously high fixed costs in planes, equipment, inventory, people, and systems. With his low value adding, that made Burr a Mercantilist.

But at People's Express, Burr took a very low-cost approach relative to other airlines. Burr's idea was to reduce *operating* costs to a then-unthinkable level. People's Express launched unparalleled low fares in the new era of deregulation. He stripped the product and service to its barest essentials to be able to survive on lower gross margins.

How does a company survive with high fixed costs and ultra-low gross margins? It doesn't. People's Express was eventually put into bankruptcy and liquidated. Burr had no way to meet the negative earnings gap created through this difficult combination of low value adding and high resource utilization.

Burr appeared to have been a Discounter, and so he was, having transitioned to this financial mission from his innate Mercantilist financial signature. It was a good idea. But his new financial mission of Discounter simply did not jibe with the reality of high capital intensity. He was more comfortable with the Mercantilist model. He could never actually exit from it, despite his intellectual appreciation for its potential benefits.

Burr illustrates some nice points about the evolution of financial mission. A leader can change his financial mission but that won't necessarily make him successful. In fact, in most cases, it will not be enough.

It might appear that the Trader can easily become a Discounter, because all she has to do is to change her resource utilization behavior. But this still requires major behavioral change. If she can achieve it, however, she has definitely improved her financial mission status. It might also seem possible for a Trader to become a Consolidator, but the transformation is just as difficult.

The best outcome for the Trader would be to become an Arbitrageur, but this is extremely unlikely. All in all, the Trader should feel successful if she can make it to Discounter or Consolidator status.

Of the Traders we studied, a few more were able to correct than the Mercantilists. One such example is Case 9, CEO of a services company. Case 9 started off in a large company as a salesperson who became very successful. He was a medium-level spender and was not too concerned about product details. He was low in value adding. So he was a Trader.

Frustrated with large-company bureaucracy, Case 9 resigned to start his own business. Sales grew quickly but the company always lost money, just as we would expect from a Trader. His company was acquired by a larger company and became a division. As division manager, he spent fairly heavily but never quite managed to make profits for a division that was already low on the value-adding scale.

Then a new CEO was hired and put Case 9 on the spot—shape up or ship out. Case 9 shaped up. He began hiring people who could add value by building new services, essentially compensating for his own shortcomings. His resource utilization did not change much. He started to make money once in a while, for the first time in his life.

By this time, Case 9 was already in his late fifties. For the second time, he left a large company and again started a new business. Just as before, sales went up quickly. But this time, he actually managed to cut costs. He also made money consistently.

Case 9 had successfully made two transitions. In his first move, he changed from Band 4 to Band 3, from Trader to Consolidator. In his second transition, he moved from Band 3 to Band 2, from Consolidator to Arbitrageur. Today he is solidly, although not spectacularly, profitable. And he does occasionally revert to type, which his employees will attest to. Overall, however, his correction is remarkable.

Case 9 is unusual. He moved not one but two bands. Many more Traders actually move from Trader to Conglomerator, within the same band. For a while, they look like heroes—until reality catches up with them.

The Conglomerator is a mirror image of the Trader. His best shot is to move to Band 3 to join the Puzzlers. A transition to Venture Capitalist or Consolidator is definitely in the cards, although it still requires a major effort.

For the Conglomerator, transitioning to a Profiteer would be the best outcome. But this would require value-adding behaviors and strategies that are simply not possible for him under most circumstances. Whether he becomes a Venture Capitalist or a Consolidator depends on his particular personal financial traits and whether it is easier for him to adjust his resource utilization or his value-adding behavior.

A typical example is Case 10, who had been CEO of a rapidly growing company in the telecommunications field. He was a strong salesperson and promoter who made major investments in marketing and sales to boost sales. He was medium value adding and high resource utilization—a Conglomerator.

The level of value in the product was never enough to cover expenses. After a characteristic financial pattern of stellar but short-lived growth, the company collapsed and was liquidated.

So Case 10 went out and promptly started a new investment company, committed to learning from his mistakes. Down went his resource utilization, even within the enterprises he invested in. His value adding did not change. Now he was a Consolidator. Although not the brass ring, it was much better than before. The last time we had contact with him, his style was still mutating to increase value-added elements, and he showed some signs of becoming a Profiteer—or at least heading in that direction. He may never make it there, but his financial mission has definitely improved.

Evolution of the Puzzler Financial Missions

The Discounter has only one real choice to truly improve her financial mission—become an Arbitrageur. This requires a higher level of value adding and a move from Band 3 to Band 2. Although possible, very few actually make the transition.

Her other choice is to become a Consolidator, which is still a difficult feat. To make the shift, a Discounter has to increase her resource utilization *and* her value adding. But to become a Consolidator is really a zero-sum option. It will not gain her or her company anything in the long term, unless there are specific strategic reasons to do so. In the short term, it may appear as though she has improved the company's chances although intrinsically she has not.

This explains why so few Discounters succeed. There is a great need for major behavior modification. But although challenging, it can and does happen. Just look at Warren Buffett, who turned Berkshire Hathaway from a Discounter financial mission to an investment vehicle. Kmart, the most famous example of a Discounter culture, may be transitioning to the same strategy.[1] Its current CEO, Edward Lampert, appears to be transitioning the company into an investment vehicle similar in concept to Berkshire Hathaway.

Most Discounters are much more similar to Home Depot under its leader, Bob Nardelli. His strategy is to take Home Depot somewhat upmarket. If it is successful, it will end up an Arbitrageur; if less so, he will end up as a Consolidator, with the same profit quality as a Discounter, in Band 3.

The Consolidator can move to Band 2, a very acceptable transition, and become a Profiteer or an Arbitrageur. Consolidators can become honorable members of the Surplus style, although they have to be determined to do so.

Case 11, the CEO of an investment company, is an example of a Consolidator. He had a financial background and was not a visionary. He was also certainly not oriented to high value adding, although he was not a commodity type, either. In the resource utilization area, he was in the middle.

When Case 11 bought out a large company, he did what he could to make it profitable. However, he lacked value-adding capabilities and the ability to reduce its resource utilization. As a result, an acquisition that could have gone in either direction went in neither. It could have transitioned to becoming either an Arbitrageur or a Profiteer financial mission. But with Case 11, a Consolidator, at the helm, neither was possible.

The Venture Capitalist faces the same situation as the Discounter. He can either transition to Band 2 to become a Profiteer by changing resource utilization behavior or drop his commitment to value adding and become a Consolidator. While either of these changes may not gain much over the long term, they will make him appear to be a more responsive leader to his investors and stockholders by adopting less risky corporate behaviors.

Paul Allen, Bill Gates's ex-partner, is a Venture Capitalist in transition. His best choice for transition is to Band 2 from the Puzzler band. To be truly successful, however, he needs to become a Profiteer. If he fails, he will become a Consolidator.

All in all, this works well for him. But note that such an evolution does not actually improve the overall financial performance of his enterprise. If he becomes a Consolidator, he will just appear to have made things better.

Steve Jobs is a well-known Venture Capitalist who has successfully become a Profiteer. For him, this way was easier because it required no change in his value-adding behavior—witness the iPod—but it took some commitment to reducing resource utilization.

Evolution of the Surplus Financial Missions

Once a leader has a Surplus style, it might appear that she has no need to correct. Her company is already intrinsically profitable, but it still may face challenges that require compensation on her part.

For instance, the leader may shift to a company in a different market or industry. She may move to a company selling a different type of product or service. She may simply want to make more money, although that is probably the least likely reason for the Surplus leader's transition to a different financial mission.

A shift to higher resource utilization or lower value adding can serve a variety of legitimate strategic corporate purposes, despite a short-term negative effect on profits. The company may have decided to buy market share with lower margin products. It may have made several acquisitions and wish to adopt the financial mission of an acquiree. It may have entered a new business. It may have decided that the only way it can compete effectively is to move upmarket.

Thus, the financial mission of a Surplus leader can and does evolve as needed. And making these transitions may be just as difficult for her as for a Deficit or Puzzler leader.

A Profiteer is often a gifted corporate steward. In theory, with just a bit of effort, a Profiteer can become a Buccaneer. But this is not very likely, as Buccaneers are in a class of their own. Frequently company founders, they view themselves as owners, not as stewards.

More likely, if there is any transition, the Profiteer will become an Arbitrageur. This can happen particularly when a leader decides to abandon value adding as a pure competitive tactic and to move down-market to lower pricing and margins. It is still a change for him because it requires shifts in both components of the financial signature. But for a Profiteer's enterprise, this shift will not result in any increases in profitability or profit quality.

A good example of a Profiteer is John Chambers of Cisco. He has spent all of his life in large enterprises, having started at IBM. He has a propensity for high value adding and a medium level of resource utilization.

Cisco has never been able to get to the levels of sustained financial performance of a Microsoft. Chambers will never be a Buccaneer. It is also pretty unlikely that Cisco could compete in the lower value-added segments of the market, at least while Chambers is at the helm. He is simply not constructed that way. Once routers and the like become a commodity, which is in process, Cisco will need an Arbitrageur leader.

A Buccaneer is as unlikely to transition to being a Profiteer as the reverse. But it can still happen, particularly if the leader is determined. He can move to Band 2 by adopting a Profiteer or an Arbitrageur financial mission.

The financial mission of a Buccaneer is built on a style of high value adding, which gives him the ability to make bold business strokes that result in his company's characteristically fast growth patterns. The shift to becoming an Arbitrageur or a Profiteer will not be painless. But it is feasible for the Buccaneer, particularly if the market demands it and his leadership position is at stake.

An interesting study in this regard is Henry Ford. He transitioned between three financial missions in his lifetime, spanning three bands. He started off as a Venture Capitalist and failed in three enterprises before he started Ford. At that stage, he transitioned to a Buccaneer. The Model T was uniquely high value adding and uniquely low cost. It was said that Ford was so stingy he used to weigh piles of paper to estimate their accounts receivable.

As the market for automobiles transitioned into a mature market, Ford adopted an Arbitrageur financial mission. He deliberately reduced value adding so that he could drop costs even further. He did this in response to the threat of strengthening competitors, such as General Motors, and was relatively successful.

The Arbitrageur is the mirror image of the Profiteer. To move up the value-adding scale takes behaviors with which she is not familiar. She feels uncomfortable with higher levels of risk and higher resource utilization.

On the other hand, if the Arbitrageur chooses the Profiteer financial mission, it does not represent an increase in profit quality. This leader may often take this route because, at least from the perspective of outsiders, it may well appear to be a better mission.

That's why Ben and Jerry's ice cream was never able to become a really successful enterprise. True, they had a great brand name. But the two partners, Ben Cohen and Jerry Greenfield, were both Arbitrageurs. And they brought in another Arbitrageur, Chico Lager, as CEO.

Ben and Jerry's resource utilization was always low. Their value adding was medium—certainly not a commodity, but not blindingly original, either. The collective financial missions of the three leaders were not able to transition to a Buccaneer mission; they were tapped out in terms of creativity. To become Profiteers, they would have had to increase resource utilization, and they did not have the collective stomach to do that.

As a result, although a very promising idea, Ben and Jerry's did not really make it as an independent enterprise. Their Arbitrageur financial mission left them with only slow-rising profitability. The enterprise was sold and now is part of a larger company.

Why Financial Missions Evolve

Leaders have several reasons to transition their financial mission. First and foremost, they may want to improve the profitability of their enterprise. Second, leaders may transition their financial mission to cope with external circumstances, such as unexpected events and trends.

In doing so, leaders may create a gap between what their financial signature is and what it needs to be. This is really a gap between what they are comfortable with and what they have to do. But remaining a leader generally requires correction and transitioning to other financial missions. This is true of Surplus types but especially true of Deficit and Puzzler styles.

Unfortunately, as we have shown, many of the feasible transitions do not result in an increase in real profitability. The tragedy is that many leaders simply cannot make the transitions that will result in material changes to financial performance.

Many of these leaders will realize that they need to change their financial mission. Some will also intuitively realize that they cannot make the required behavioral changes to achieve improved profitability and profit quality. Some of these will take the easy way out by transitioning within a mission band rather than moving to a more profitable band. From the outside, this will look like a change in financial mission that benefits the enterprise. But once it becomes clear that it will not result in any material change, the leader will usually exit. Outsiders will simply conclude that the change in enterprise strategy did not work for reasons they are unsure of.

Lessons of the Financial Mission Bands for Emerging Leaders

Emerging leaders are often unaware of their capabilities—both of their financial signature and of their potential to transition to another financial mission.

This has numerous implications. In looking for a new job or accepting a promotion, a leader might be tempted by compensation or other benefits to take on a position that requires a new financial mission that he is simply incapable of adopting. Or to meet the challenges of external competition, an organization might need a new financial mission with which the leader is unfamiliar. They might adopt a strategy that looks good on paper but requires behavioral changes that they simply cannot make.

The five mission bands hold three major lessons for leaders at all levels:

- The bands show the paths of change that are theoretically feasible for a leader's personal characteristics and thus should be pursued.
- The bands show paths of change that may not yield improved financial performance and should be generally avoided unless there is a specific reason to take them.
- The bands show the paths of change that are unrealistic and should never be attempted.

The last lesson may be the most important. By showing a leader what is unrealistic in terms of change, we can save him wasted effort and put his particular psychological assets to the most efficient and effective use.

Notes

1 R. Berner, "The Next Warren Buffett," *Business Week*, November 22, 2004, 145–152.

How a Financial Mission Evolves

This chapter demonstrated that:

- A business leader should aim to achieve a corrected outcome, that is, to compensate for his or her financial signature.

- A business leader who succeeds either has a financial signature that is congruent with enterprise and market conditions or has been able to compensate for the adverse effects of his or her financial signature.

- A business leader tends to correct with age and previous business leadership experience. Being in a partnership has a significantly positive effect on his or her ability to correct.

- A leader can correct any financial mission, even a Surplus financial style.

- Evolution of the financial missions is subject to the five mission bands.

- If a leader transitions within a band, he or she may appear to have changed, but the transition will not actually result in an improvement in the enterprise's long-term profitability.

- To achieve a true change in an enterprise's profit quality, a leader needs to transition between bands, toward the Surplus styles—not within them.

- The greater the transition required, up or down the value-adding or the resource utilization scale, the less likely it is that a leader will succeed.

- Even a Surplus leader will have difficulty moving from her natural financial mission to another.

- A leader with a Deficit financial mission can correct and improve his profits as long as he follows a road map that is appropriate to his particular financial signature and psychological circumstances.

Top Two Takeaways
- In taking a promotion or new job that involves transitioning your financial mission, stay within personally realistic limits.

- You can make major transitions as long as you are very self-aware and determined.

SELF-DEVELOPMENT EXERCISE

For your particular financial signature, write down all of the possible paths that will allow you to transition to a new financial mission that will bring about a true increase in the profit quality of your enterprise.

Possible Paths

1. _____

2. _____

3. _____

4. _____

Now choose one or more paths that are feasible for you. Write them down.

Feasible Paths

1. _____

2. _____

3. _____

4. _____

Now write down three reasons why you would take these routes rather than another path.

1. _____

2. _____

3. _____

ASSESSING YOUR
FINANCIAL SIGNATURE

Stories abound about the early lives of prominent business leaders, many of whom set up lemonade stands. Warren Buffett, Bill Gates, and Michael Dell, for example, gained early experience managing their lemonade stands, then went on to start serious enterprises while in college.

If you had business interests at that age, what did they reveal about your financial signature? What role did you play in the creating and success of My Lemonade Stand, Inc.? Did you want to make the lemonade or sell it? Did you have a yen for finding vastly improved lemonade, or did you focus instead on finding new customers for it? Did you find the least expensive ingredients, or did you instead go for the best taste? Your answers to each of these questions are already providing clear signals of your financial signature.

The lemonade stand is a metaphor for how you approach all matters financial. The decisions you make in your private life often clearly portray your financial signature.

What is your approach to money? Do you invest aggressively or conservatively? What type of asset allocation is in your mutual funds or 401K accounts? Are you a strong saver or a heavy investor? Do you aim for high-risk investments with high rewards, or the reverse? If you have a lot of money, do you hoard it away, or do you splurge? How important is it to you that others see that you have expensive possessions? Each of these provides clear signals of your financial signature.

How about your approach to building things? Are you a mad inventor? An inveterate tinkerer? Do you want to give the world a new way of doing things? Or do you simply want to make tons of money?

You can use all of these and other criteria to describe yourself and your friends. These are all financial traits that influence most of your waking hours, reflecting aspects of your innate financial signature.

Childhood and Financial Signature

If you wish to understand your financial signature, ask your parents. They often understand it better than anyone.

The behavior you exhibit as a child is often more revealing of your natural and innate self than what you do when you are older. As you mature, you learn how to compensate for or disguise your natural habits. You may even forget your natural ways of acting, so successful have your compensation strategies been.

When you read biographies, try focusing on the accounts of the main protagonist as a child. This may often seem to be irrelevant, but it is not. As the saying goes, the child is father to the man. You may learn much more about the real essence of a leader from reading about his childhood than by reading accounts of his contemporaries at a later age.

Take Sandy Weill of Citigroup again. Weill is often seen as a gregarious and extroverted person. But the accounts of his childhood and even of his early professional life paint him as retiring and averse to public get-togethers. He comes across as introverted and shy—a far cry from the person you see today.

Apparently, Weill made enormous personal adjustments. He compensated for many of his early and innate behaviors in several constructive ways. Seeing him now, you might be inclined to think that his current behaviors are innate even though his biography suggests otherwise. This information helps you recognize his true financial signature.

The same pattern is evident in the biographies of leaders such as Michael Dell, Bill Gates, and Warren Buffett. Each of these men exhibited early behaviors that drove the financial performance of the enterprises they went on to create. In each of their cases, you can learn more about their natural style from their early life than from the later stage when experience, observer bias, and straight-out public relations take over and distort your perspective.

Why Assess Your Financial Signature?

There are six main reasons to discover your financial signature:

- You are in a leadership position and want to improve the performance of your organization.
- You are starting a new enterprise or a new organization within your existing enterprise.
- You wish to be promoted into a general management or even a CEO position.
- You are in middle management and wish to align yourself with the financial culture of your enterprise.
- You are buying into a company or small business.
- You are just POC—plain old curious.

Let's take a look at each of these reasons.

Improving the Performance of the Enterprise

If you are like many of our clients at the Perth Leadership Institute, you may be a business leader, often early stage or midstage, who wants to discover what your financial signature means for improving your enterprise's performance. And, if needed, you want to know how you can compensate for this signature and what types of strategies are required to do this.

Very few business leaders have an ideal financial signature, so this is usually a constructive exercise. It often provides a new way of thinking about your effect on your enterprise's financial performance.

Starting a New Enterprise or Organization

If you are like others of our clients, you may be a founder and CEO of a new enterprise, either independent or within a larger organization. You may have had no formal business education or even experience. You may be an executive in a larger company who wishes to leave and start your own company.

Or perhaps you are a brilliant, technical person who has developed a new product or technology and wonders how to proceed from there. Or you may have had plenty of business experience but not at the CEO or top-executive level.

In most of these cases, you have had little or no knowledge of general management. Moreover, conventional leadership approaches are not going to help much, either.

Understanding your financial signature will give you some insight as to how your financial style will likely affect the financial performance of your company. It will also give you insight regarding what strategies you need to compensate for your financial signature and what types of people to bring in to assist you.

Seeking Promotion to General Management

You may be a manager or other executive who aspires to the corner office. Maybe you wish to be divisional president, general manager, or some other senior position having profit-and-loss responsibility.

There are few, if any, courses on how to prepare for general management as distinct from middle, or functional, management. Probably the best way to prepare for general management is to become the understudy of a top executive, where you are forced to assimilate the experience of the leader. Appreciating how resource utilization and value adding play into valuation is a skill that all successful top executives have learned, although they may not have formalized it in this way.

Or perhaps you have another motive—you wonder how you compare to your executive peers. How common or otherwise is your financial signature? What happens to the enterprises headed up by a business leader with the same type of financial signature you have? How do other business leaders with your financial signature correct for their styles? Are you competitive with other executives who are bidding for the same position?

These are normal questions. We are all interested in how we compare to others, but we need a common yardstick. The financial signature provides that yardstick. Once you can measure yourself against others, it can provide new approaches for you to improve your performance.

Aligning with the Organization

If you are like many middle-level executives, you may never wish to become the leader of an enterprise. But you certainly wish to be aligned with the financial culture of your organization. You need a tool to help you assess your own financial signature to understand how to align it with the financial culture of your organization.

A lack of alignment between personal financial signature and the financial culture of the organization may be the cause of many problems if you are a middle executive. While you may feel that you are performing poorly, in fact, you maybe very competent; you may simply have a financial signature that is different from your organization's mission.

Understanding the causes of this misalignment can make you much more effective. It will make your organization more effective, too. In the Appendix, we provide a self-assessment tool to help you align your financial signature with that of your organization.

Buying into a Company or Small Business

Although often overlooked, if you buy a franchise, or just a small business, you are part of a huge category of leaders. If you are like many of these leaders, you are an expatriate from corporate America with little or no general management experience.

Although as a franchisee you will often get training from the franchisor or owner, you will rarely receive leadership guidance. And if you are an entrepreneur starting from scratch, without the backing of a franchisor, you will receive even less training—often none at all.

Like many of these entrepreneurs, your small business is probably your pension. When you retire, you will sell the business to fund your retirement. The higher the market value, the bigger your retirement fund. So you have a very practical reason to understand your financial signature.

Being POC—Plain Old Curious

Plain old curiosity is a valid reason for exploring your financial signature. Curiosity drives much of our behavior, and it is a legitimate motive if you are seeking a change but are not sure where to go.

A variety of individuals fit in this category. You may be a student who is still very unsure of what you should do and what you would be good at. You may be a dissatisfied midcareer worker or professional. Perhaps you are newly retired and looking for a new field to enter.

By learning your financial signature, you will understand your potential better. You can prepare to maximize your value and performance for whatever you do next.

Understanding your financial signature can further your personal development as much as attending a yoga class or taking an ecotour in Costa Rica. It may also turn out to be more profitable for you.

Uncovering Your Financial Signature

Having seen how to discover the financial signature of a business leader, it should be easy to apply to yourself, right? Probably not. As we have discussed, you are now subject to the very issues of self-discovery and self-awareness that we all encounter when it comes to discovering yourself.

The most accurate way to discover your financial signature is to complete the Financial Outcome Assessment offered by the Perth Leadership Institute. There are other ways too, which can be used by themselves or in conjunction with the online assessment. On their own, however, they will not be as accurate as the formal online assessment.

To assess yourself using the material in this book, you may want to ask others to help you. They may be more objective and can provide a way of checking your answers.

Methods you can use include:

1. Friends
2. Mentors and coaches
3. Work performance appraisals
4. 360-degree performance reviews

Let's look more closely at each of these methods.

Friends

Probably the best source of feedback on your financial signature is from friends. Make sure they know that you want them to be objective and that there is no wrong answer. You may be seeking their feedback either to help improve your own performance as a leader. Or you may want them to assess your potential for such a position.

Your friends know you well. They can give you feedback on the two components of financial signature very quickly. Once you have that information, you can quickly read off your financial mission.

Mentors and Coaches

If you are like many well-known business leaders, you may now have your own leadership coach to help you improve your leadership capabilities. It is almost de rigueur in some organizations.

Having a private coach for leadership might once have been regarded as something to conceal, rather like the old view of having a private therapist. These days, we know differently, and having such a mentor or coach can be a wonderful addition to your career options and performance.

Many larger enterprises have a formal mentoring system. In such cases, you should introduce your mentor to the book and ask her to help rate you according to our scales. If you are not in such an enterprise or situation, consider finding yourself a mentor, someone older and more experienced, someone whom you respect and like, someone who can provide a level of wisdom that you hope to possess yourself some day.

An assessment of your organization's financial mission, such as the one in the Appendix, may be a valuable way to find a mentor and open up the mentoring relationship. It will allow you to approach a potential mentor with a request for his or her assistance in applying the assessment. In fact, the best way to use this book is with your current coach or mentor or one whom you will find as a result of reading and using this book.

Work Performance Appraisals

You probably receive formal performance appraisals at work, especially if you work in a larger enterprise.

Although it is unlikely that the structure of such appraisals is the same as those used here, they may have components that are sufficiently similar to allow you to apply some of their results to the scales used in this book.

In addition, you may want to ask your supervisor or human resources contact to provide you with feedback along the lines of our components. Your boss may be very happy—and even flattered—to provide additional feedback on your performance potential. Remember to tell whoever is helping you that there is no right or wrong answer.

If your organization does not have a formal performance appraisal system, consider asking your supervisor to appraise you using our two components. Most should be more than willing to oblige.

360-Degree Performance Reviews

Recently, 360-degree performance reviews have become very popular in larger companies. A 360-degree review is simply organized feedback from multiple sources who are familiar with the performance of the person being appraised. They can use a variety of instruments, depending on the objectives of the review.[1]

If your organization uses 360-degree performance reviews, some of the questions may overlap with some of the scales used in this book. This could help you apply that feedback to some of our scales. If the questions do not overlap, or if you have no 360-degree reviews, you could ask your human resources people to arrange for a quick 360-degree review using the scales presented in this book.

Depending on your position, you may not be comfortable with a full 360-degree review. In that case, it makes sense to hire a consultant to work through the scales with you, using limited feedback from certain sources, including friends or even family. In these cases, the consultant or coach is essentially acting as one of the feedback sources. The consultant may not be as good a source as others who know you well, but the resulting review may still be of great value.

Conducting Your Self-Assessment

You are now in a position to start your self-assessment. You can do this in five simple steps:

1. First, select the people you want to participate in your assessment. If you want to do it by yourself, just proceed to the next step.

2. Both you and your appraisers should indicate what you each see as your positioning on both of the two financial signature components. (See Chapter 3.)

3. These responses will provide you with a self-rating of your financial signature, which you have learned about throughout this book.

4. Now go to the Appendix. The assessment there will help you decide whether you are aligned with the financial mission of your enterprise.

5. If you wish to have a formal assessment of your financial signature conducted, contact perthleadership.org.

As you will see later, finding your financial mission is the beginning, not the end of the exercise. Once you know your financial signature, you can decide how to develop your own leadership potential using the information and approaches in this book.

Difficulties of Discovering Your Financial Signature

Our model defines nine financial signatures and missions. Clearly, much is involved in discovering what yours are. The two components of financial signatures also reveal themselves in different ways to different people in different situations.

Of the two components, resource utilization is the easier one to determine because you can look at your spending and saving patterns on both a professional and personal level.

Value adding is a much harder component to assess. For starters, you may not understand exactly what is meant by value adding. To get around this, you respond to questions about your behavior.

But it is still often difficult to answer this one for yourself. After all, if you are like most people, you think of yourself as creative. The only way to answer this one is to again look at your actual behavior—that which is overt and available.

In the process of assessing your financial signature, you may also discover information about yourself that you don't want to know. To find, for example, that you characteristically are a high spender with low value-adding tendencies could be painful and is certainly not flattering.

On the other hand, if you are stepping into a leadership position, isn't it better to know this up front? You can now compensate for these traits. You and your enterprise can now be successful instead of failing.

Too many executives enter a leadership path and fail as leaders. Had they known about these personal financial styles beforehand, they may have succeeded. Their enterprises could have performed better and their shareholders could have profited handsomely as a result. Not only is knowledge power, but it is the key to success.

If you are honest with yourself, you stand to make tremendous gains. You have made the first step in self-improvement as a leader. You now can construct a road map for how to achieve the profitable financial performance for your enterprise that it and its shareholders deserve.

Notes

1 See W. Tornow and M. London, *Maximizing the Value of 360-Degree Feedback: A Process for Successful Individual and Organizational Development*, San Francisco: Jossey-Bass, 1998.

Assessing Your Own Financial Signature

This chapter demonstrated that:

▶ A person's early behavior in dealing with money and business may tell us much about his or her financial signature.

▶ There are six reasons to discover your financial signature:

1. You are already in a leadership position and want to improve the performance of your organization.

2. You are starting a new enterprise or a new organization within your existing enterprise.

3. You wish to be promoted into a general management or even a CEO position.

4. You wish to align yourself with the financial signature of your enterprise.

5. You are buying into a company.

6. POC—plain old curiosity.

▶ You can conduct a self-assessment or ask outside observers to rate you on the same scales to discover your financial signature.

▶ You can use the quick organizational alignment self-assessment in the Appendix or use the more formal assessment of your financial signature from perthleadership.org.

Top Two Takeaways

▶ Find a coach or mentor to help you interpret your financial signature and, if necessary, to determine how you can transition to compensate for it.

▶ Ask several colleagues to conduct a 360-degree assessment of you, using the financial signature as the basis.

SELF-DEVELOPMENT EXERCISE

Do I need to transition to a different financial mission? Why?

_____

_____

_____

_____

_____

_____

_____

_____

_____

_____

_____

_____

_____

_____

_____

_____

Are there external reasons, such as competition or a change in the market, that dictate a change in my financial mission?

_____

_____

_____

_____

_____

_____

_____

_____

_____

_____

_____

_____

_____

_____

_____

Are there any internal organizational reasons why I should
transition to a different financial mission?

_____

_____

_____

_____

_____

_____

_____

_____

_____

_____

_____

_____

_____

_____

_____

IMPROVING
PERFORMANCE

Therefore are thousands of books about improving a company's financial performance. All of them can be divided into two broad categories: books about financial strategies and books about leadership.

Books about financial strategies include those about capital and its costs, improving resource utilization, adding value, improving the supply chain, and so on. Leadership books address how to make leadership better in some way. Techniques can include improving individual competencies, improving vision, execution, and communication, and the like.

Financial strategy books can be very valuable, but they ignore one critical factor—the leader's financial signature. The authors of these books presume that all of the recommended strategies are equally applicable to all types of leaders. Of course, this is simply not the case. Depending on their financial signature, different leaders need different strategies. In fact, strategies that might be good for one leader could be harmful for another.

Leadership books can also provide helpful insights for leaders regarding how to improve their performance. But they have a major deficiency as well. They do not draw any formal link between leadership and financial outcome. The presumption is that if the leader takes actions to improve his leadership style, positive financial consequences will then automatically follow. However, the specific mechanism by which this will occur is seldom discussed.

Business strategies are like newly discovered pharmaceuticals. In certain individuals, they have a very positive clinical outcome, while in others they have no result or even a negative clinical outcome. The drug has huge value to some people, but it could kill others.

Changing the Financial Mission

Let's review the difference between a financial signature and financial mission. A financial signature is innate—it never changes. A financial mission is the behavior that results from that financial signature, and it *can* change. But whether it changes, or to what degree, depends entirely on the leader herself.

This gives us hope. A leader with a Deficit financial mission has the possibility of compensating enough that her financial mission can approach or, in some circumstances, even become a Surplus financial mission. In other words, having a Deficit or Puzzler style, which is what most people have, does not necessarily mean that she cannot become an effective leader. True, she is unlikely to become a Bill Gates or a Sandy Weill. But then, I am sure she knew that anyway.

A leader who fails sometimes realizes where she went wrong—but generally only after the fact. Once she comes to this realization, however, it is almost always too late to help the company she is leading.

The aim of this book is to accelerate this learning process. If leaders can jump ahead of the curve, they can figure out what to do before they fail. Then they can apply those techniques that suit their particular genetic makeup.

Strategies for Improving Financial Performance

Financial performance is a short-term issue. Market value is its long-term consequence. Good financial performance does not always necessarily lead to a rising market value, as many factors can intervene.

There are several strategies for improving the financial performance of an organization. These include:

- Financial leadership assessment
- Differentiated leadership development
- Personalized intervention
- Synchronized leader and team missions
- Matched financial mission and company strategy
- Personalized strategies

Let's look at each of these strategies in turn.

Financial Leadership Assessment

Our research shows that effective leadership must incorporate a financial performance dimension. The term *assessment* refers to formal methods to identify the financial signature and the financial mission of the leader, as without this information, we do not have a place to start to improve the enterprise's profitability. By *financial assessment*, we mean an instrument that takes enterprise outcome and profitability into account.

Differentiated Leadership Development

The crux of the model in this book is that a financial signature leads to a characteristic financial mission. The three financial styles are Deficit, Surplus, and Puzzler, each of which has a characteristic pattern of profitability outcome.

In developing leadership training, we cannot treat the three financial styles the same way. They are fundamentally different and reflect radically different approaches to creating market value; thus, each needs a different type of program, as shown in Figure 9.1.

Deficit styles need a distinct program. Because leaders with these financial traits are intrinsically unprofitable, they need the strongest intervention and require active and formal programs. After all, their natural tendency is to go in the wrong direction for the enterprise over the long term.

The chance of failure for Deficit leaders is greater because the distance to the Surplus style is larger. But

Figure 9.1 Emerging leader development.

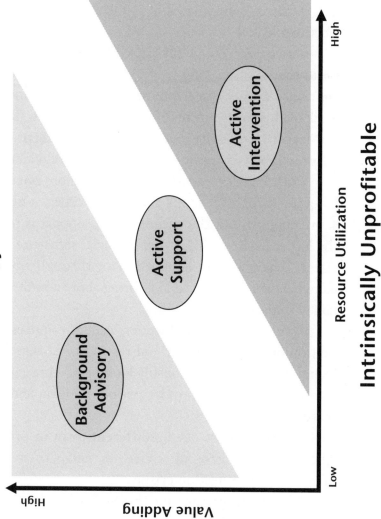

they could move to a Puzzler style, which can often result in a positive outcome. This intervention is certainly worthwhile.

Active intervention for Deficit leaders requires a program that is fairly long (at least two years), regular (at least once a week), and intensive (at least two hours per week). This program may sound burdensome. But if it can lead to a positive outcome for the enterprise, the effort will be very positive in terms of shareholder value.

With Puzzler leaders, the program does not have to be quite as forceful as for the Deficit types. They need active support, but the nature of the support is to make the leader aware of his or her financial signature and its effect. Then we can support them through the more incremental changes needed to bring about a positive, sustained impact on profitability.

Active support for Puzzler leaders requires intervention but not the power and regularity of that for the Deficit types. We are probably looking at a program that is formal and monthly over a period of a couple of years as well.

Surplus leaders need a different form of program. They need background advice to nudge them gently rather than to transition crisply.

It is tempting to assume that Surplus leaders are perfect and need no support. However, they may not be suited to the particular enterprise or market they are in and thus could still fail. And, even if they were well-suited at one time, they may need to change their financial mission as external circumstances, market evolution, and the stage of enterprise development also change.

Thus, although the program for Surplus leaders may not need to be intensive, there is still a reason for it to exist. Having an adviser in the background can provide the vital function of making them aware of market and other shifts that may render their financial mission less appropriate.

Many leaders might balk at the programs we have described above. But for their shareholders, if the outcome is positive, the effort is worthwhile. After all, this is leadership development in its purest form. It is carried out for the benefit of these shareholders and has practical fiscal consequences. We should not ask any less of any leader.

If hubris steps in to prevent such development programs, then the leader may not be self-aware and flexible enough to cope with any change at all. In that case, the owners of the enterprise should, rightly, worry. A leader should be prepared to make this sort of sacrifice for the common good. For many leaders, this will be a self-development exercise that can only increase his personal, as well as his professional, value. This alone should make it worthwhile.

Personalized Intervention

In Chapter 6, we examined how the different financial missions evolve. Each of the nine missions evolves in the same basic way, but results in different choices for the leader.

Interventions should be tailored to the particular financial mission. In most cases, the ultimate aim is to enable the leader to migrate to the mission band immediately above and to the left of the one she currently occupies. This is achievable with effort and a personalized program.

A few leaders may be able to migrate more than one band. Working with leaders individually enables us to see which of them could fit into this category and then develop an even more carefully tailored program. The endeavor may be achievable but require even more effort.

For some leaders, the best choice may be to transition to a different financial mission but still remain within the same band. True, this may appear a null strategy for the leader. But other circumstances may argue for such a strategy. These include competition, a change in the market, or other needs to reposition the enterprise in the market. This strategy requires a careful examination of these circumstances and then an appropriate intervention program.

Synchronized Leader and Team Missions

We have already made the point that, to achieve good financial performance, the financial mission of the leader must be synchronized with that of his team. There is no point in having different missions.

The process of synchronization includes several components. These include identifying the financial signatures and financial missions of the leader and the senior executive teams, identifying the intervention programs required, implementing those programs, and monitoring the programs and soliciting feedback to ensure that they are achieving their purposes.

Synchronization can be a hard or a soft process. In the hands of a Sandy Weill or an Al Dunlap, for example, it is a hard process. In the hands of a Colman Mockler, of Gillette, it is a soft process. Much depends on the culture and history of the organization.

Leaders who use a hard process are not necessarily being ruthless. In fact, most of these leaders are synchronizing the financial missions of the leadership team. When Al Dunlap and Sandy Weill were pruning the ranks, they were intuitively synchronizing the financial missions with their own. These leaders know that unless they have total synchronization, they will not succeed in achieving their overall market value goals for their organization.

We also have to view the soft process of synchronization in this light. The soft process may nurture widespread organizational support by demonstrating that the leadership really cares about bringing everyone along for the ride. But to the extent that an organization needs everyone to pull together quickly, this process may just not be appropriate. Colman Mockler's Gillette was forced into paying off Irwin Jacobs, a notorious corporate raider, under this soft process. Gillette ultimately incurred deep debt, which depressed Gillette's market value for many years. It is not enough to see whether a leader builds a supportive culture. We have to assess the effect of the mission synchronization process on the enterprise's financial performance and valuation trajectory.

Neither the hard nor the soft process is necessarily right or wrong. Financial mission synchronization can be successful either way. In assessing what is the right choice, however, the speed of execution and efficiency of the strategy need to be weighed against other considerations such as cultural and social factors.

Matched Financial Mission and Company Strategy

Company strategy covers many areas. The level of maturity of the market, the type of product or service, and the enterprise's own stage of evolution all come into play. Choosing the leaders and teams with the correct financial missions requires consideration of all these aspects.

If the financial missions of the leaders, their employees, and their teams are not synchronized with these strategies and factors, there will be a gap. This gap will lead to a less-than-optimal financial performance—and the possibility of that performance worsening.

Personalized Strategies

Financial strategies to achieve particular corporate ends are well known. However, to be successful, these strategies need to be customized according to the financial signature and mission of the leader.

Categorizing the fundamental types of financial improvement strategies gives us a framework to tailor them for leaders with different financial missions. There are only four basic types of financial improvement strategy:

• **Value-adding strategy:** Improve value-adding behavior and gross margins (because this financial mission is generally well controlled in the area of resource efficiency and utilization).

- **Resource efficiency strategy:** Improve resource efficiency and cut expenses, broadly defined (because this financial mission is generally well controlled in the area of product value added).
- **Composite strategy:** Improve both gross margins and resource efficiency (because this financial mission generally has problems in both areas).
- **Optimizing strategy:** Reduce value adding and simultaneously increase resource utilization.

Each of these strategies matches to a particular type of financial mission, as shown in Figure 9.2.

Value-Adding Strategies. These strategies apply to leaders who, at first sight, already appear to be very successful at creating value. These leaders are the Arbitrageur and the Discounter. They run tightly managed enterprises that create value through sustainable earnings streams and through tight management of margins. They often have innovative logistics and distribution systems. They may be widely cited for their cost-consciousness and internal controls. It may appear to be difficult for such leaders to improve, but they have two major vulnerabilities:

- **Short term:** Resources for investment are limited, leading to problems in increasing the value of products and services. This can in turn lead to declining gross margins that are masked by good earnings due to tight cost controls.
- **Long term:** Investment is insufficient to keep the enterprise competitive in its products and services. Eventually, the enterprise loses market share and its gross margins fall so much that the effect on its earnings cannot be

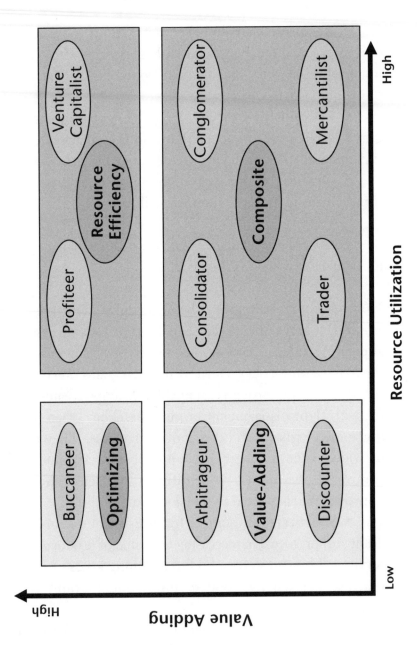

FIGURE 9.2 The four profitability correction strategies.

compensated for by cost controls, leading to earnings problems.

Resource Efficiency Strategies. These strategies apply to leaders who, at first sight, also appear to be very successful at creating value. These leaders are the Profiteer and the Venture Capitalist. They have high–value-added products and/or services that lead their industry and their market. They compete very well on features and function and, indeed, may be the leader in their area. They are innovative and create new industry directions. They may be widely cited for their path-breaking accomplishments. However, these leaders also have two major vulnerabilities:

- **Short term:** The resource outlays needed for their particular strategy are high. This inevitably leads to earnings issues and even issues of enterprise survival.
- **Long term:** Even though the enterprise's products may lead the field, from the perspective of features and function, they do not lead the market. They risk being marginalized or even failing.

Composite Strategies. Several of the financial missions—the Consolidator, the Conglomerator, the Trader, and the Mercantilist—have intrinsic vulnerabilities in both value-adding and resource efficiency areas. These leaders are particularly at risk and require strategies that meet both of these sets of needs.

Other leaders may not have a major vulnerability in one of the areas but still need some reminders. Many leaders who are fine in the value-adding area may still need a refresher occasionally. They may have strayed from their competencies under the pressure of work, crisis, or even personal pressures.

Yet other leaders who are successful in both areas can still improve. And leaders who are aware that they have a particular strength can still increase this strength even further—providing that they focus even more on their characteristic vulnerabilities.

These types of leaders have several major vulnerabilities, including:

- **Short term—value adding:** Resources for investment are limited, leading to problems in increasing the value of products and services. This can lead to declining gross margins that are masked by good earnings due to tight cost controls.
- **Short term—resource efficiency:** Even though the enterprise is well managed, its level of resource utilization surpasses its current level of product or service value added.
- **Long term:** The enterprise's investment is insufficient to keep its products and services competitive. Eventually the enterprise loses market share and its gross margins fall so much that the effect on its earnings cannot be compensated for by cost controls.

Optimizing Strategies. These strategies apply to leaders who, at first sight, appear to have it all—the Buccaneers. They have high–value-added products and low outlays. It may appear to be difficult for such leaders to improve because they are already pursuing high value-adding strategies for products or services and low resource utilization strategies.

However, this leader has three major vulnerabilities:

• **Short term—value-adding:** In the value-adding area, high value added often produces some complacency, which results in customer dissatisfaction and either loss of customers or a poor public image. Competitors become a growing threat.

• **Short term—resource utilization:** A strong focus on reducing resource outlays in the resource utilization area leads to deficits in the areas of product quality and customer support. This can lead to customer disaffection and support for competitors, which can erode competitive position and lower potential valuation.

• **Long term:** The company's products have been so successful that it becomes complacent and loses sight of ways to innovate and to develop new products, which leads to competitive issues in the future.

Thus, leaders of all types, even leaders who have an apparently optimal financial style, can benefit from refining their techniques to better serve their enterprise.

Suggested Techniques

There are a huge number of techniques that could be adopted within each strategy. Here are just a few to get you started.

Value-adding strategies comprise some of these techniques:

- Develop a gross margin improvement plan.
- Introduce a sales compensation plan based on gross margins rather than revenues.
- Carry out a competitive analysis to show how competitors pick up points of gross margin.
- Prepare a quality improvement plan.
- Work with marketing to identify how different product strategies can pick up additional points of gross margin.
- Identify best practices by operating unit that result in higher gross margins.
- Carry out a product feature/function analysis.
- Cut the costs of the goods sold.
- Develop a new pricing strategy.
- Carry out a competitive pricing analysis.

Resource efficiency strategies include some of the following ideas:

- Set up a product investment committee to produce a formal product investment plan.
- Set formal goals for each operational area— sales, research and development, and administrative—in terms of allowable expenses as a proportion of revenues. Indicate percentage limits that will decline as revenue increases.
- Include expense goals in compensation plans and provide bonuses for meeting those goals.

- Set up an internal bidding system that allows groups of employees to propose how they can achieve strategic product goals at lower cost than other groups, and then give the winners the project to complete.
- Set up a formal budgeting process.
- Set up a formal MBO (management by objectives) process, which sets formal objectives and the means to achieve them.
- Set up a balanced scorecard process in which metrics are identified that measure how well the company performs in specific areas.

Composite strategies might cover some of the following techniques:

- Conduct a product/service value analysis.
- Set up a product or service value strategy committee to develop immediate recommendations for improving value added.
- Conduct a competitive analysis focused on the market leaders and differences between their product/service value and your own.
- Develop a gross margin improvement plan.
- Introduce a sales compensation plan based on gross margins rather than revenues.
- Carry out a competitive analysis to show how competitors pick up points of gross margin.
- Prepare a quality improvement plan.
- Develop a new pricing strategy.
- Carry out a competitive pricing analysis.

- Set up a product investment committee to produce a formal investment plan for products.
- Set formal goals for each operational area—sales, research and development, and administrative—in terms of allowable expenses as a proportion of revenue. Indicate percentage limits that will decline as revenue increases.
- Include expense goals in compensation plans and provide bonuses for meeting those goals.

Optimization strategies could include:

- Prepare to relax value-adding strategies and to allow gross margins to decline a little.
- Set up a committee and process to identify new areas for investment that will produce new products.
- Set up a committee to review areas where it would be prudent to increase expenses and investment.
- Use a Buccaneer's surplus to increase customer support outlays and effectiveness, as well as product or service quality.
- Increase spending on public relations.
- Introduce customer relations initiatives, such as outreach to disaffected customers.

Using these ideas as a starting point, you can probably come up with creative strategies to improve your company's performance.

The Golden Rule

This chapter has set out a series of financial approaches based on the financial signature model. But be careful not to treat these choices as straitjackets. Remember that resource utilization and value adding need to be appropriate to the circumstances—this is the golden rule.

Financial strategies that are based on extremes may be headed for disaster even if they conform to the principles presented here. For example, Buccaneers may well have, mathematically speaking, the most favorable earnings gap of any financial mission but still have a problem. They may have to deliberately shrink this gap to reduce potentially negative customer and public reactions that this success is at their expense.

Your innate financial signature may drive you to ignore the golden rule. Mercantilists are that way because their innate personal financial traits drive them to spend more than is appropriate for the circumstances. Discounters go for low value adding for the same reason, even when it is not appropriate.

There is a choice, revealed by the financial signature model. Overlay the golden rule on top of your choices to find out the best strategy to maximize your financial performance.

Improving Profitability Performance

This chapter demonstrated that:

▶ The improvement of financial performance is dependent on the following factors:

1. Assessing the financial mission of the leader and the leadership team

2. Differentiating between the different types of development programs that are needed by the leader, based on his or her financial mission

3. Personalizing the intervention based on the precise financial mission of the leader and identifying the most effective and feasible choices for him or her regarding his or her ideal financial mission

4. Synchronizing the financial missions of the leaders and his or her team

5. Matching the financial mission of the leadership team with the enterprise's strategy and external circumstances

6. Personalizing strategies to the particular leader implementing them

▶ The golden rule—that resource utilization and value adding need to be appropriate to the circumstances—will help a leader find his or her best strategy to optimize the company's performance.

Top Two Takeaways

▶ Strategies for profitability improvement should be matched to your financial mission.

▶ Making a transition to a more appropriate financial mission requires a development program tailored specifically to you.

SELF-DEVELOPMENT EXERCISE

Write down which of the four profitability improvement strategies best applies to you.

_____

_____

_____

_____

_____

_____

_____

In your current position, what particular techniques that you saw at the end of the chapter could benefit you in improving your profitability approach?

_____

_____

_____

_____

_____

What types of training assistance do you think would most help you in making the transition to a more profitable financial mission?

- Training seminar
- Focused coaching
- Mentoring
- Formal training course in the area of leadership
- Formal training course in financial techniques for leaders
- Other

Write down what you think is the best mix of approaches for you.

_____

_____

_____

_____

_____

_____

_____

_____

_____

FINANCIAL
SIGNATURE AND
STREET VALUE

STREET CRED:
THE NINE MARKET
VALUE TRAJECTORIES

Market value is really the only objective measure for assessing a company's financial performance. To link a business leader's personal financial traits to company outcome, market value must be its proxy.

A leader's financial signature leads to a characteristic financial mission. Each financial mission, in turn, leads to a characteristic market value direction—improving or declining.

Relative Market Value

At any particular time, a company's fundamental market value can be assessed using any number of the normal valuation metrics, such as price-to-earnings (P/E)—the ratio of the stock price to its dividend, price-to-sales, net worth, various cash flow ratios, and so on. A company can also be compared to the known value of other enterprises in its industry—the comparables method. Using any of these methods, we can arrive at an estimate of market value. This allows us to assess the relative performance of the company. However, these will be only imperfect measures. Depending on the state of the market, these methods may over- or underestimate the enterprise's underlying value.

Absolute Value or Relative Value?

There is a difference between the absolute value of a company and its relative value. The absolute value is a measurement on a well-defined scale, such as a P/E of 25 or a PSR (price-to-sales ratio) of 2.3. The relative value of a company refers to how its value compares to other companies in its industry.

A company may have a value that is more or less than the average, or it may be some proportion of the average, such as being worth 50 percent more than the average company in its industry. This perspective allows us to compare enterprises in a wide variety of industries where values vary significantly between them. For example, it may not make much sense to compare one company that has increased its value from a P/E of 15 to 25 with another that has increased its value from a P/E of 4 to 8. But if the average P/E of a company in its industry is respectively 10 and 3, we can use the common yardstick of the percentage change in P/E to compare each company directly. The average company's value will always stay constant relative to the competition.

For the purposes of this book, we will use relative value. It allows us to standardize our measure of outcomes between enterprises in different industries and provides a way to compare the consequences of one particular financial signature with another across industries and enterprises.

Public or Nonprofit Organizations?

Market value is a concept normally associated with private enterprises. But a public or nonprofit organization also has a fundamental value. It has products or services, customers, often sales and shareholders, and, in the case of government, voters. The same concepts of financial signature and value can be used to assess the effect of leadership on such organizations as well.

There are a variety of potential market value measures we can devise for public and nonprofit organizations, including resource utilization per employee, expenses as a proportion of customer revenues, revenue growth of customers to whom they provide services, total gross margins, and gross margin per employee. The data exists to conduct all of these measurements, which can help enhance leadership development in these types of organizations.

Enterprise Cycles and Stages of Evolution

Market value is not a static concept—it is constantly changing. It will change in the short run due to cyclical factors, and it will change in the long run due to fundamental factors. The fundamental factors come into play as the enterprise evolves from birth to growth to decline to death—identifiable phases in which a company's value undergoes characteristic transitions.

The stage of the company's evolution is important. Each enterprise has a series of valuation trajectories or pathways, and each of these pathways will be linked to an identifiable phase that the enterprise occupies. Some enterprises may go through a linear evolution from birth to death. Others may undergo repeated cycles of decline and rebirth, with characteristic upticks and declines connected with each cycle of decline and rebirth.

Leadership has its own effect on market value. In developing a framework for assessing market value, time is a crucial factor. In what follows, we will usually speak of market value as a value trajectory or pathway because it is less meaningful and useful to speak of market value just at one particular point.

Nine Fundamental Market Value Outcomes

Corporate market values seem to vary inexplicably. For one or many enterprises, they may even appear to be chaotic.

Yet we can at least identify the fundamental market value trajectories of any enterprise. Enterprises can undergo, over a period of years, a characteristic pattern of growing value, declining value, and value that both grows and declines within the same cycle.

Looking beyond the chaos and volatility of the stock markets, we see nine basic patterns. These are:

Growth Valuation Outcomes
- Gently Rising Tide outcome
- Fast-Rising Tide outcome
- High Plateau outcome

Decline Valuation Outcomes
- Dying Swan outcome
- Terminal Patient outcome
- Quasar outcome

Growth-and-Decline Outcomes
- Balloon outcome
- Brown Dwarf outcome
- Steady State outcome

Growth Outcomes

Companies gain market value at different rates. The styles of these growth rates can be described as a Gently Rising Tide, a Fast-Rising Tide, and a High Plateau.

Gently Rising Tide

The Gently Rising Tide is a very familiar pattern. It occurs in enterprises with a decent market position, a good management team, stable management and leadership, and probably a good, but not stellar, product or service. While aggressive investors might prefer something a bit more exciting, this is a good general stock because it may well pay a dividend and is not likely to go out of business suddenly. Most utilities, insurance, and banking organizations fall into this category.

Before it was taken over by Kenneth Lay and Jeff Skilling, Enron was an example of a Gently Rising Tide. Before Lay, Enron had turned in steady but not spectacular growth.

Fast-Rising Tide

The Fast-Rising Tide is a company everyone wants to own stock in, although, by definition, it is pretty hard to pick in advance. Typically, such enterprises have a high gross margin product relative to the competition that is well differentiated and has little or no competition. The enterprise may not pay a dividend, but few sharesholders care because the stock is appreciating so well.

The most common examples of Fast-Rising Tide enterprises in recent years have been technology companies or those involved in online retailing. These are the stars we all hear about. Microsoft is a classic example of this type, and, several years ago, IBM was another. During the dot-com era, we had companies like Juniper and Checkpoint in the technology sector, and eBay and Amazon in online retailing. Fast-Rising Tide enterprises are often a product of their times but, as we will see, they are also a product of their leaders.

High Plateau

The High Plateau outcome is just what one would expect. The market value of the company grows to a certain point and then plateaus, never increasing beyond that point. The enterprise has reached its maximum potential. This is not an attractive enterprise for investors because there is no stock appreciation and a declining dividend, if any at all.

There are plenty of examples of High Plateau companies, including IBM before Lou Gerstner and AT&T before the telecom bust. Enterprises in a consolidating industry are the ones most likely to be on such a path.

Decline Outcomes

Unfortunately, companies also lose market value. A company's decline will fit into one of three patterns—the Dying Swan, the Terminal Patient, or the Quasar.

Dying Swan

The Dying Swan outcome for an enterprise is pretty familiar. Dying Swans often have a product characterized by low gross margins in a mature market and in a competitive, even cutthroat, industry. Lack of investment in new products has left the enterprise vulnerable to emerging competition, and there is unfortunately nowhere to go but down.

The Dying Swan enterprise is almost theatrical in its value pathway. Like the dying swan of musical fame, its dying process is long, tortuous, and tragic. It still has a brand name and some residual customer loyalty that it can continue to exploit, but even these are at declining levels. AT&T was a Dying Swan. It could not beat the rap, no matter how hard it tried.

Many Dying Swans can avoid their fate by being acquired, as did AT&T. Another good example is Digital Equipment Corporation, which missed the PC phase and was doomed to extinction. It avoided that fate by being acquired by Compaq, which was later acquired by Hewlett-Packard when Compaq itself entered the Dying Swan phase.

Terminal Patient

The Terminal Patient is probably the most common of all the value pathways. Most enterprises die, usually at an early stage.

We notice Terminal Patients when they are large enterprises because they have a major effect on employment and the competition, while the small ones that die barely catch our eye. There are a variety of reasons, competitive and otherwise, for their passing, which we will discuss later.

Some enterprises in this category appear to miss this stage by being acquired, usually as an asset rather than as a stock sale. In reality, as an operating enterprise, the company is effectively dead before it is acquired.

Once Terminal Patient enterprises die, they pass from memory. In the technology area, such once-strong enterprises as Wang, Data General, and Convergent Technology are no more.

Quasar

The Quasar is a star that is normally invisible but suddenly, for no apparent reason, undergoes a spectacular celestial fireworks display, then sheds its light and reverts to its original, invisible state.

Quasar enterprises gain possibly more media attention than any other type. Enterprises and leaders that were hitherto unknown become instant celebrities. They are, literally, a beacon to the ambitious. Their fast descent into ignominy has a tragic aspect, too, that equally attracts attention. If we could find out what made them tick, we could all be rich. If we could discern what led them to fail, we would never be poor.

There are numerous examples of Quasar enterprises, including many from the boom-then-bust dot-com era. Some of them, such as Polaroid or Parmalat, lasted longer than others. Others, such as People's Express, lasted only a short time.

Sometimes, Quasars return to what they were originally. For example, Vivendi survived its near-death experience under Jean-Marie Messier. Often Quasars are the perpetrators of huge frauds, such as Enron, HealthSouth, and WorldCom, indicating that Quasar status can be a function of both the market and the leader.

Growth-and-Decline Outcomes

Some companies both grow and decline in more or less predictable patterns. These patterns include the Balloon, the Brown Dwarf, and the Steady State.

Balloon

The Balloon outcome is a fairly unpredictable one. As its name implies, the increase in market value arrives right at the very end, if at all. Very often, the ending market value for a Balloon outcome is preceded by an early spike. Investors become enamored of an apparently unique product with high gross margins that has the potential to dominate an industry. But usually such a spike is relatively short lived, as the sales and development cycles are long and it becomes almost impossible for the enterprise to live up to investor expectations. If the enterprise makes it, however, there will be a major payoff.

An example of a Balloon valuation is Imclone, but many biotech companies fit the profile. Imclone's long development was characterized by an early spike when it went public, followed by a long decline. News that its product was about to be rejected by the FDA led to a long downturn. Imclone finally emerged with an effective drug and its stock price climbed accordingly.

Brown Dwarf

The Brown Dwarf is another type of star. Astronomers believe a Brown Dwarf was once a big healthy celestial object. But it used up all of its nuclear fuel, leaving virtually no energy, and shrank to a tiny fraction of its original size. Yet it refuses to die. Such is the fate of many enterprises today.

Once in a while, for reasons no one quite understands, a Brown Dwarf star can erupt again, breaking out of the Brown Dwarf cycle. This is why we call it a Growth-and-Decline path.

Brown Dwarf enterprises often had a cutting-edge technology or product at one time. That product still has a use, although no longer for most people. Singer Sewing Machine is a good example of such an enterprise. It still exists, but it is a shadow of its original size and influence.

Berkshire Hathaway, originally acquired by Warren Buffett, was also a Brown Dwarf, a textile company that had seen better days but still had a small market left. It had the good fortune to be taken over by Buffett. But even Buffett could not restore Berkshire Hathaway's fortunes and ended up making it the holding company for his investments.

Steady State

A Steady State value pathway is as likely to go up as down. On average, however, it remains unchanged. An enterprise whose market value continues to stay at around the same level—average for its industry—is a Steady State company.

If we can understand what drives a Steady State enterprise to never change its market value, it will show us what to avoid. In fact, this pathway has a lot to do with the financial signature of its leader.

Market Value Cycles

Each of the nine value trajectories that an enterprise can have is part of a broader cycle. The enterprise may be nearing the end of its life, or it may be just beginning. More likely, the enterprise is transitioning between phases. For example, it may have just divested itself of a leader who has led it to a Terminal Patient pathway and is wondering what to do next.

Figure 10.1 shows a number of options for pathways companies can take. Logically, an enterprise could transition within each of the Growth, Decline, and Growth-and-Decline value pathways. We call these the small-circle market value transitions. In this pattern, the enterprise never leaves its particular type of pathway. It just cycles within the Decline modes—an unhappy but not uncommon phenomenon. Or it can cycle between the Growth modes.

An enterprise can also cycle between Growth and Decline modes, between Decline and Steady State (or stagnancy) modes, or even between Growth and Steady State modes. Of course, these small circles could also change chaotically. In that case, we need to understand what shifted the organization from its particular orbit.

Some enterprises follow larger shifts, such as from a Fast-Rising Tide to a Terminal Patient, over a period of

FIGURE 10.1 Market value cycles.

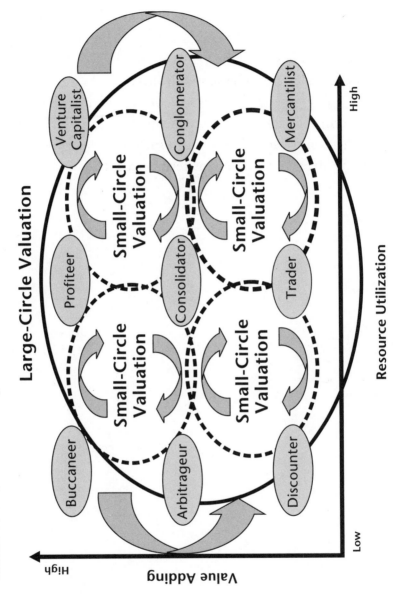

a few years. This happens especially during boom-bust cycles such as the dot-com era or when companies change leaders. These patterns, also shown in Figure 10.1, are the large-circle valuation pathways.

The financial signature of a leader will indicate whether she takes her company into small- or large-circle valuation trajectories. This, in turn, will determine if her company can achieve long-term success.

The Nine Market Value Trajectories

This chapter demonstrated that:

▶ Classifying market value trajectories gives us a way to assess the effect of leaders with different financial signatures.

▶ A company's market value should be assessed relative to other companies in its industry.

▶ There are three basic market value patterns—the growth, decline, and growth-and-decline patterns.

▶ There are nine market value trajectories, which can be used to categorize an enterprise's market value outcomes for the purposes of linking them with the leader's financial signature.

▶ These pathways can also occur sequentially over the life cycle of an enterprise.

▶ These pathways can occur in different sequences for different enterprises at different stages of evolution.

Top Two Takeaways

▶ Enterprise market value outcomes can be categorized into nine pathways.

▶ Assessing the market value of an enterprise relative to other enterprises in its industry allows you to compare a leader's effect within his or her company.

SELF-DEVELOPMENT EXERCISE

What has happened to the market value of the enterprise you are currently involved in over the past three years?

- Increased
- Decreased
- Stayed the same

To what extent were you responsible for this change?

_____

_____

_____

_____

_____

To the extent that you were responsible for this change, how did your financial traits affect this change?

_____

_____

_____

_____

_____

CHAPTER 11

FINANCIAL MISSION AND VALUE TRAJECTORY

The market value trajectory of each of the nine financial missions is determined by the earnings gap and the capital engine (see Chapter 4). A positive earnings gap indicates a potential for earnings, while a negative earnings gap indicates a tendency toward losses. When the earnings gap is positive, the value trajectory will be one of the Growth types. When it is negative, the trajectory will be one of the Decline types. And when it is zero, it will be one of the Growth-and-Decline types. These trajectories are shown in Figure 11.1.

Each of the nine financial missions corresponds with one of the nine market value trajectories.

Growth Valuation Trajectories
- **Buccaneer:** there is a large positive earnings gap because value adding is high and resource utilization is low; this leads to a high-growth pathway, that of the Fast-Rising Tide.

FIGURE 11.1 Growth and decline value trajectories.

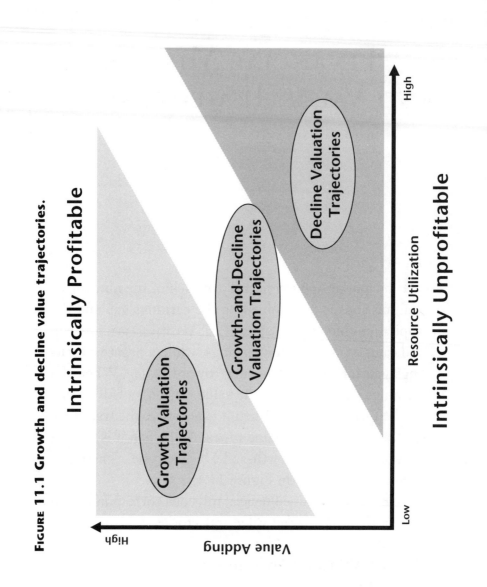

- **Profiteer:** there is a medium-sized positive value gap because there is high value adding and medium resource utilization; this leads to fair growth and a Gently Rising Tide value trajectory.
- **Arbitrageur:** there is a small positive value gap because value adding is medium and resource utilization is low; this leads to relatively lower growth, which stabilizes at some point, and to a High Plateau value trajectory.

Decline Valuation Trajectories

- **Mercantilist:** there is a large negative earnings gap because resource utilization is high while value adding is low; this leads to rapid decline and to a Terminal Patient value trajectory.
- **Conglomerator:** there is a small negative earnings gap because resource utilization is high and value adding is medium; this leads to declining growth relative to the industry and to a Quasar value pathway.
- **Trader:** there is a medium-sized negative earnings gap because resource utilization is medium while value adding is low; this leads to a long, slow decline and to a Dying Swan value trajectory.

Growth-and-Decline Trajectories

- **Venture Capitalist:** there is no earnings gap because both value adding and resource utilization are high; this means a roll of the dice or a Balloon value pathway.
- **Consolidator:** there is no earnings gap because both resource utilization and value adding are at medium

levels; this is also a roll of the dice, which, on average, means a Steady State trajectory.

• **Discounter:** there is no earnings gap because both resource utilization and value adding are low; there is an indeterminate outcome—on average, the company will fail due to a lack of investments, leading to the Brown Dwarf value trajectory.

The linkage between value path and financial mission is shown in Figure 11.2. This figure demonstrates more clearly how the nine value trajectories correspond to the nine financial missions.

Positive Versus Negative Value Trajectories

The positive and negative trajectories can be plotted on the same diagram as that of the financial mission of the leader, as shown in Figure 11.3.

Clearly, it would be best for a company if the leader's financial signature and mission were in the upper third of the diagram. We would not generally want a leader whose financial mission was situated in the lower third of the diagram. Nor would we really want one whose financial mission was one of the three on the diagonal—this pathway is indeterminate at best and too likely to take on a negative trajectory at least half of the time.

What does this diagram tell us about the financial signatures we should be looking for? Long term, all other

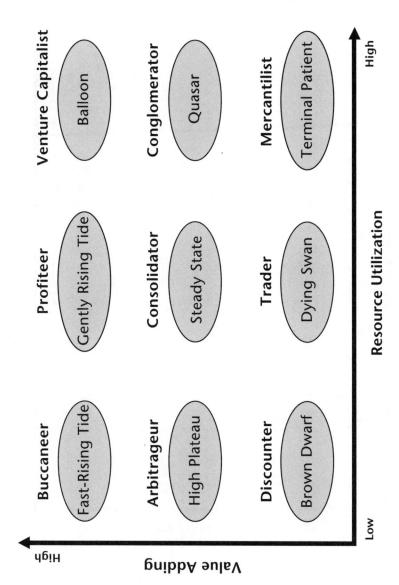

FIGURE 11.2 Value trajectories and financial mission.

FIGURE 11.3 Good versus bad valuation trajectories.

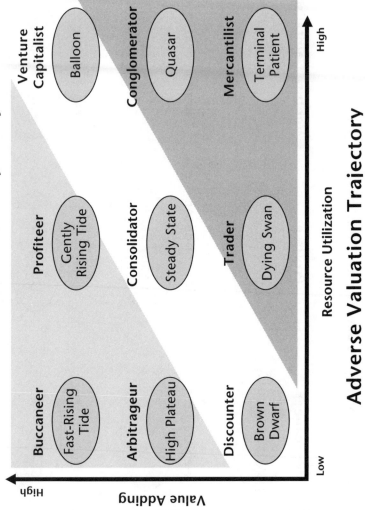

things being equal, the particular financial signature of a leader will predispose him to particular outcomes. If his traits are predisposed to positive value pathways, then that is what is more likely to occur, other things being equal. And if these traits are predisposed to negative outcomes, the same holds true. Of course, if the leader is aware of his personal financial style, he can correct for it.

The leaders who are favored by the nature of their financial signature are the Profiteer, the Buccaneer, and the Arbitrageur. Those who are not favored at all are the Conglomerator, the Mercantilist, and the Trader. And the leaders whose outcomes are in doubt are the Venture Capitalist, the Consolidator, and the Discounter.

Keep in mind that a leader with a good level of self-awareness and determination can avoid many of the negative outcomes. A leader without this level of self-awareness and determination will probably not.

Profit and Organizational Needs

Organizations and boards expect their leaders to make profits and to increase shareholder value. But there are many ways to make a profit. For example, one can do it with high margins and medium costs or with medium margins and low costs, to mention just two of the many options.

Any leader has a variety of ways to make a profit. But the method she is most likely to choose is dependent on her innate financial signature. While this may indeed deliver the desired profit, the method may not fit the needs of the organization. While a medium margin/low cost combination may achieve the same raw profit numbers that another approach may yield, it will yield a different organizational effect and a different kind of valuation than, say, a high margin/medium cost approach.

The various combinations open to a CEO to deliver a profit essentially result in different market value quality. What do we mean by this?

Market value quality is all about sustainability. Two apparently identical values that differ in sustainability will actually result in a difference in real company value. And the quality of market value, what investment bankers would probably call valuation quality, counts.

For example, Al Dunlap of Sunbeam delivered the profit level his masters asked for but, as we see later, they probably did not like the type of market value that came with it. They were looking for sustainable market value. Lower market value quality means the same numerical value, but with a lower probability of it being sustained over the long term.

Market value quality is highly dependent on the leader's financial signature. As demonstrated in Figure 11.4, quality increases from bottom right to top left. For any given level of profit, market value quality will always increase in this direction.

We have analyzed numerous published accounts and biographies to assess the financial signature of some well-known leaders. The link between financial signature and

Figure 11.4 Market value quality and financial signature.

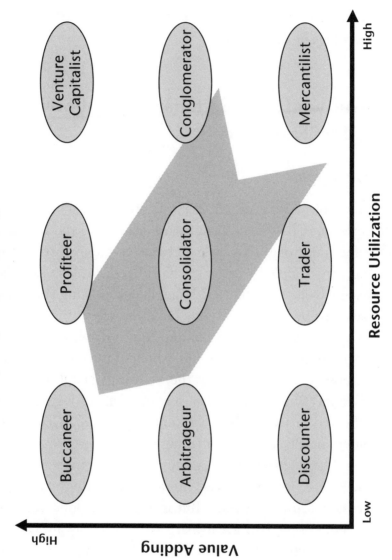

value trajectory becomes even clearer by examining examples of these leaders.

The Venture Capitalist and Balloon Value Trajectory

Steve Jobs

Steve Jobs is an excellent example of a leader with a Venture Capitalist financial signature leading to the Balloon value trajectory. This style is characterized by infrequent big wins coupled with much more frequent losses. This results from high value-adding tendencies being counterbalanced by a propensity for high resource utilization.

Jobs's best-known creation, Apple, demonstrates his financial signature well. It has exhibited the Balloon value trajectory characteristic of the Venture Capital financial mission. But we can also see his financial signature reflected in two of his other enterprises, NEXT Computer and Pixar, the filmmaking company.

These enterprises share a common characteristic—they were potentially very high value-adding and high gross margin businesses. But in each case, Jobs overinvested.[1] Apple had great margins, but it was always an expensive company to run. The NEXT computer was an aesthetic breakthrough but a commercial failure, precipitated by Jobs's ultra-high expense style.

Today, Apple, after several brushes with death, is still a leader in computing. Like the original Macintosh computer, the iPod is a high-value must-have that is part technology, part fashion accessory. However, the company's expenses are a bit more restrained. And Pixar is the leader in its field.

How do we explain Jobs's recent success with Apple? Jobs is an example of a corrected leader. His uncorrected financial signature is that of the Venture Capitalist. But his near-failure the first time round in Apple and his subsequent ouster, together with his failure at NEXT and the early near-death experience of Pixar, finally led him to correct. Jobs has now converted his financial mission into that of the Profiteer, namely, high value adding and medium expense.

What about the value trajectory of these enterprises? In Jobs's first tenure at Apple, it was essentially a Balloon type. Its value trajectory languished for a period until it suddenly took off when the Mac hit the market. Apple became a market value star.

NEXT's value trajectory was potentially a Balloon value, too. Its value, albeit private, was always relatively low. It never succeeded nor achieved the market value that could have occurred in happier, albeit statistically unusual, circumstances.

Pixar's value was another potential Balloon value trajectory. Its value was low for many years while Jobs and his staff diligently toiled at developing a new animation technology that would revolutionize filmmaking. When it finally broke through, its value skyrocketed almost overnight, becoming the quintessential Balloon value trajectory.

In his second tenure at Apple, Jobs achieved a major turnaround. This time around, however, rather than a Balloon value, he first achieved a Gently Rising Tide value trajectory. His metamorphosis into a Profiteer led him to reduce expense levels—not radically as with a Buccaneer, but significantly. This resulted in a sure but unspectacular path to earnings. The iPod reflects his success in changing his financial mission to that of Buccaneer—a Fast-Rising Tide.

The Buccaneer and Fast-Rising Tide Value Trajectory

Sandy Weill

In our studies, Buccaneers are disproportionately founders of enterprises. They are usually self-made men and women who have created an empire from scratch rather than rising through the corporate ranks.

Sandy Weill of Citigroup searched for companies that significantly exceeded the gross margins typical in the financial services industry. He took over Commercial Credit, which made consumer loans at very high rates to consumers who had no other place to go—what some people call loan-sharking.[2] The bottom of the food chain, where Commercial Credit was positioned,[3] was where the highest gross margins are found.

Citigroup's acquisition of Associates was carried out for the same reason.[4] According to Alan Deutschman,

Weill ". . . nurtured a fondness for the reliable, if unglamorous, business of lending at high rates to customers most banks wouldn't let in the door. . . ."[5] And it was these high gross margins, coupled with Weill's unremitting cost control, that led to his continuing high profitability and consistently good stock price.

The value trajectory of Weill's enterprises has usually been that of the Fast-Rising Tide. When Weill has acquired enterprises, their stock price has usually then increased sharply.[6]

But there is a dark side to the Buccaneer, too, which can be seen in Citigroup's recent problems. These include its banking involvement in the Enron and Parmalat fiascos and in its being banned from the Japanese private banking market due to its flouting of Japanese laws. The aggressive financial culture of the Buccaneer can leave many victims in its wake.

The Mercantilist and Terminal Patient Value Trajectory

Dennis Kozlowski

It is unfortunate that Dennis Kozlowski is now best known for his legal problems and the charge that he looted Tyco. Putting aside the criminal charges, he is a good example of a Mercantilist.

Tyco was comprised of many different types of enterprises. These included fire alarms, healthcare, electronics, and insurance companies. In amassing so many businesses, Kozlowski attempted to rival Jack Welch of General Electric. The problem was that these companies were all unrelated. And unlike Welch, Kozlowski never added any value to any of them. He was basically a financial engineer.

In fact, it would even be true to say that Kozlowski actually subtracted value from the company. Tyco post-Kozlowski is worth much less than it was before him. It lost money on many of its acquisitions and its stockholders certainly suffered.

On the resource utilization side, Kozlowski was high. He was infamous for his extravagant style (remember the gladiator party for his wife?). He bought expensive art, apartments, and such with company money. Besides being illegal, his personal spending patterns reflected those in his business life.

The Mercantilist has a Terminal Patient value trajectory, due to the negative earnings gap between value adding and resource utilization. Tyco is still in business, and the new CEO has made valiant efforts to turn the company around. But had Kozlowski remained, there is little doubt that a Terminal Patient is exactly what the company would have become.

The Mercantilist has to cope with the likelihood of a Terminal Patient trajectory. He can either take it on the chin, or he can try to beat the rap. The vast majority of Mercantilist leaders are ethical individuals, but some are tempted to take the less ethical way out. For the small minority who are ethically challenged, the Mercantilist mission embodies a negative earnings gap that may lead them to unethical behavior to avoid the Terminal Patient outcome. This is the dark side of the Mercantilist.

Sometimes the Mercantilist financial mission may not appear to lead to the Terminal Patient value trajectory. The company may be so large that a government may not allow it to fail. Just look at Alstom, Thomson, Credit Lyonnais, Chrysler, and the airline bailouts. These, in effect, are Terminal Patient outcomes, too; they are just disguised by the bailouts.

The Discounter and Brown Dwarf Value Trajectory

Bernard Ebbers

Bernard Ebbers is a fascinating example of how a Discounter can go so forcefully down the wrong path. His Discounter characteristics can be seen early in his life. Ebbers's background reveals that he had little interest or capacity in building new types of products and services. He essentially retailed the services of others. He was comfortable being entrepreneurial and low value adding.

Ebbers started off his empire-building career in LDDS (Long Distance Discount Service), a discount provider of long-distance discount telephone services. LDDS was the perfect reflection of the Discounter financial signature. It owned no lines itself; it simply rented bandwidth from others to keep its costs very low.

Over the years, LDDS made many acquisitions. In the beginning, these acquisitions were other telephone carriers with a similar mind-set. But by the mid-1990s, LDDS gravitated toward telephone carriers that owned real assets, particularly fiber optics.

This change in the LDDS (now WorldCom) model meant that Ebbers had transitioned from his original Discounter model to a Mercantilist financial mission. He was still low value adding, but with high expenses. By the mid-1990s, the writing was already on the wall for the Discounter model in the telecommunications industry. WorldCom was entering the beginning stages of a Brown Dwarf value trajectory characteristic of a Discounter. Thus, it is no surprise that WorldCom started to transition to the Mercantilist model. It appeared to Ebbers that it was a way out of the Discounter's market value dilemma.

But the Mercantilist model implied no new value added. It just changed the cost structure. In fact, WorldCom's fundamental position had dramatically worsened by transitioning to the Mercantilist mission—the worst value trajectory of any of the financial signatures. This was obscured, deliberately or otherwise, by the ever-bigger acquisitions WorldCom was making, culminating in the MCI acquisition.

From the outside, this appeared to have been the ultimate triumph. In hindsight, however, it marked the culmination of a deeply flawed Mercantilist financial mission.

Ebbers swapped one bad valuation trajectory for an even worse one—a Brown Dwarf for a Terminal Patient trajectory. While the long-term outcome would be even worse, in the short term, the results would appear to be spectacular. It would keep the stockholders buying and the investors investing, which, no doubt, was the point. Eventually, however, WorldCom filed for bankruptcy, just as our model predicts.

The Achilles' heel of the Discounter is that the low costs required to operate profitably mitigate against making any investments, whether in sales and marketing or in distribution. In the vast majority of cases, Discounters are in mature industries where they can make money only for a limited amount of time. But the lack of surplus for investments eventually dooms their business to a Brown Dwarf trajectory. Only Discounters who are first movers, such as a Wal-Mart, where the earnings are so high that they can provide enough surplus to keep the first-mover advantage, will be exempt from this outcome.

Notes

1 A. Deutschman, *The Second Coming of Steve Jobs*, New York: Broadway Books, 2000, 142.

2 M. Langley, *Tearing Down the Walls: How Sandy Weill Fought His Way to the Top of the Financial World . . . and Then Nearly Lost It All*, New York: Simon and Schuster, 2003, 113.

3 Ibid., 117.

4 Ibid., 368.

5 Ibid., 367.

6 Ibid., 201, 211.

Financial Mission and Value Trajectory

This chapter demonstrated that:

▶ Each of the nine financial missions is associated with a characteristic market value trajectory through the mechanism of the earnings gap.

▶ Each of the nine financial missions is associated with either a positive, a negative, or an indeterminate value trajectory.

Top Two Takeaways

▶ You will affect the market value of your enterprise in your own characteristic way—become aware of it now so that you know what to expect.

▶ If you change your financial mission, you will also change your value trajectory.

SELF-DEVELOPMENT EXERCISE

What is the value trajectory associated with your financial mission?

_____

_____

_____

_____

_____

Does it need to change to result in a better outcome for your organization?

_____

_____

_____

_____

_____

If so, how does it need to change?

_____

_____

_____

_____

_____

_____

Do you have the capability to transition your financial mission
to the optimum mission for your desired value trajectory
outcome?

_____

_____

_____

_____

_____

_____

How Financial
Mission Drives
Business Strategy

How does the financial mission of a leader affect the business strategy of an enterprise? Do certain business strategies correspond to particular financial missions?

This chapter will examine these issues from several different perspectives. First, are different types of leaders more effective in different types of market structures? Second, are some financial missions more suited to certain types of industries? That is, does a leader's financial mission make her more effective in certain types of markets? Third, are certain leaders more effective with certain types of market-positioning strategies?

These are all important questions. They challenge the conventional assumption that good leaders are, generally speaking, good for any type of market structure, positioning, industry, or product. But even if you accept that leaders need to be better matched to companies based on their financial mission, there is still no accepted model for how to do it.

Financial Signature and Market Structure

Markets come in three flavors—fragmented, consolidating, or consolidated/mature. All markets will possess one of these three structures or be somewhere on the continuum between them.

- **Fragmented markets:** these markets have many players. The products and services are relatively new, with more new types emerging frequently. The market is evolving quickly, and there is a high degree of uncertainty. New players constantly arise and often fail. Market growth is very high, often well above 100 percent per year.
- **Consolidating markets:** these have reached a stage where there are relatively few players. There are no new products, only product extensions. Market growth has slowed to about 10 percent to 30 percent. The majority of small enterprises in the field have failed. However, there are still a small number, usually five to ten, that have significant market share.
- **Consolidated/mature markets:** these markets have reached an end point. Only one or two products and companies dominate the market. There is little or no product innovation and few new products or enterprises appear because the market is simply too hard to penetrate; the major players virtually own the market. As a result, the market is stagnant, with little growth, until a new paradigm comes along and destroys it.

Each of these markets has different characteristics that require different business strategies to survive and prosper.

Fragmented Markets

Fragmented markets favor leaders with high value-adding financial missions—the Venture Capitalist, the Profiteer, and the Buccaneer. These leaders aim to control the market and gain a sustainable competitive advantage for their enterprise. Financial missions with low value added do not do well in these markets. They simply do not deliver enough value added to stimulate customer demand to the point of potentially dominating the market.

Even among the high value-adding leaders, there are differences. Resource utilization is a key variable. Most leaders in this category, the Venture Capitalists, will insist on a high level of resource utilization, mainly because their experience has been solely with high resource utilization enterprises. But they will struggle.

The most successful leaders in the fragmented markets are the Buccaneers because they have an intrinsically profitable financial mission. But Buccaneers are rare because of the difficulty of creating high value added with low resource utilization. Buccaneers do this, Venture Capitalists do not. Profiteers are a good second choice, offering a middle ground between the Venture Capitalist and the Buccaneer.

This provides us with an important guide to recruiting leaders in the fragmented phase. There are only two types of leader who can consistently achieve profits for the enterprise at this stage—the Buccaneer and the Profiteer. It is the job of the enterprise, the board, and its recruiters to find them. All too often, however, enterprises at the fragmented stage of market evolution recruit or are started by Venture Capitalists.

America Online (AOL) is an example of a company that could never be profitable because of the Venture Capitalist financial mission of Steve Case, its founder. True to the valuation trajectory of the Venture Capitalist, AOL ended up with a Balloon value pathway. In an effort to moderate his own intrinsically unprofitable financial signature, Steve Case brought in a second-in-command, Bob Pittman. Pittman was supposed to rein Case in and be a strong operating chief—a counterweight to Case.

What Case was essentially looking for, without knowing it, was a Profiteer, or even better, a Buccaneer. Instead, Pittman was a Conglomerator, high resource utilization and medium value adding. This was a man seeking celebrity status for whom no expense was too high. As chief operating officer, he was also responsible, with Steve Case, for the questionable accounting that erroneously inflated AOL's profits for years. AOL was doomed—at least as a profit-making entity that could increase shareholder value.

Consolidating Markets

Consolidating markets are a different animal. They require leaders with a medium value-adding financial mission. Accordingly, in these markets, we predominantly see three types of financial missions: the Conglomerator, the Consolidator, and the Arbitrageur. But of the three, only the Arbitrageur has an intrinsically profitable financial mission over the long term.

Clearly, enterprises generally need to avoid Conglomerators, who have a Deficit financial style—at least when they need someone for the longer haul. Consolidators are also not advised for the long term because they are, at best, a gamble. Only Arbitrageurs offer a relatively sure way of making money over the longer term.

An enterprise's chances of finding the right leader decrease at this stage of market evolution, in part because few leaders have a Surplus financial style—only one among the three medium value-adding missions. But another reason is that many leaders have been trained within relatively large enterprises accustomed to high resource utilization. Such companies are in the maturing stage of enterprise growth where cash may not be a problem, unlike those in the consolidating markets. Their experience may be totally wrong for the challenges the company in the consolidating market is facing.

Very often, boards select a leader who has had the type of experience likely to cause the enterprise to incur losses. Conglomerators and Consolidators look attractive to recruiters and boards but do not have the financial signature needed for the enterprise to succeed because they cannot consistently generate earnings.

Enterprises in a consolidating market need an Arbitrageur. Arbitrageurs have the appropriate level of value-added drive to lift the enterprise out of its midcycle doldrums. And their resource utilization is low enough for the enterprise to make money.

Why would the enterprise not select a leader with, say, a Buccaneer financial mission? The enterprise is already consolidating around a particular financial mission and value-adding strategy. It is highly unlikely that a new leader would do anything but create additional overheads in adding value, causing the company more harm than good. The enterprise's best option is to go with the Arbitrageur and ensure that it stays within the bounds of what is feasible for its particular level of market evolution.

One of the most famous Arbitrageurs would have to be Rupert Murdoch, who has a medium value-adding financial signature. It is not in his nature to add excessive value. Like most Arbitrageurs, he understands that too much value added can be a liability. The company can move too far ahead of what the market wants, thus reducing sales and leading to expenses that are too high to sustain until demand emerges.

Murdoch also has the Arbitrageur trait of low resource utilization—he has an intrinsically profitable financial signature. However, he is not a Buccaneer. Thus, News Corporation has not experienced the huge market value increases of, say, a Microsoft.

Many of the leaders in consolidating markets are professionals without the keen sense of minimal resource utilization that comes from being a founder. This makes them, at best, Consolidators and, more likely, Conglomerators. Boards and the enterprises they oversee need to filter these out and go for the Murdoch look-alikes.

Consolidated/Mature Markets

Mature markets are the hardest ones to find successful leaders for. They tend to filter out any leader but those with a low value-adding mission—the Discounter, the Trader, and the Mercantilist. Two of these are intrinsically unprofitable, and the third, the Discounter, is a gamble at best.

There is no intrinsically profitable financial mission for this market, so an enterprise can never expect to find the perfect leader. Here, often, the best it can do is to recruit a Discounter and hope for the best. The Discounter may or may not make it. And even if he does, the valuation trajectory is that of the Brown Dwarf, hardly an attractive outcome. While a Discounter may appear to work for a while, eventually the Decline valuation trajectory will catch up with him.

Some leaders switch to a Mercantilist financial mission. Of course, this has an even worse outcome, that of the Terminal Patient. But by raising spending considerably, such leaders often fool the market and themselves by making huge acquisitions that make it look like they are on a winning course. However, these leaders end up taking their enterprises down with them, in one form or another, so this tactic is hardly recommended.

Nor does it make sense to select a Consolidator leader. These leaders have a medium level of value adding, which is likely to be totally inappropriate for a mature market. To increase levels of value adding requires additional investment, which could be fatal to a business already generating little or no earnings surplus.

Moreover, there are cultural reasons for this strategy not to work. Employees have been selected for their ability to work within this level and will not be able to understand or digest higher value-adding strategies. Nor will they often go along with higher resource utilization because most will recoil against what they perceive to be a profligate strategy.

The mature enterprise is a real conundrum for enterprises and boards. No doubt this is why most mature enterprises usually either fail eventually or sustain themselves as Brown Dwarfs, yielding no value to their shareholders.

This is not to say that there may not be a way out of an apparent dead end. The enterprise in a mature market may still have some chance of success if it moves to a leader with an appropriate financial signature. A good example is Home Depot. When Home Depot started to slow down, even its cofounder, Arthur Blank, was unable to stem this trend. The enterprise had had a Buccaneer financial culture, but it was now entering the ranks of the Arbitrageur. With no action, it might have even entered the gravitational black hole of the Discounter, ending up as a pre–Edward Lampert Kmart.

The company appears to have made a smart choice in bringing over Bob Nardelli from General Electric to stem the flow. Nardelli was head of GE Power Systems and is renowned as an operating person rather than as a strategist. As a corporate steward, it is unlikely he is a Buccaneer; he is almost certainly a Profiteer, with the characteristics of high value adding and medium resource utilization.

Nardelli's high level of value adding has already resulted in improving gross margins at Home Depot. He is focusing on more expensive goods and solutions, albeit not high-margin products. For example, Home Depot's bestselling fan used to cost $19, now it is $199.[1] The only potential danger here is that Nardelli will try to add too much value, which will increase costs above what is required by the enterprise's optimum financial mission.

Leadership Capabilities and Market Structure

A leader's financial mission predisposes her to leading a particular type of enterprise. For each financial mission, the leader will prefer to lead an enterprise that is undergoing the particular phase of market evolution that her mission is suited to, as shown in Figure 12.1.

Leaders with a tendency toward low value adding will feel most comfortable heading an enterprise in a mature market. These enterprises will not demand that they achieve things their personal financial traits make it naturally difficult to accomplish.

Leaders with a propensity for high value adding will not feel comfortable leading an enterprise in a mature market. Their natural tendency to add more value will not be required and they will feel frustrated. Likewise, such enterprises will not appreciate their talents.

The tragic fact about financial mission is that it leads certain types of enterprises and leaders to naturally choose each other when, in most cases, they should not.

FIGURE 12.1 Financial mission and market structure.

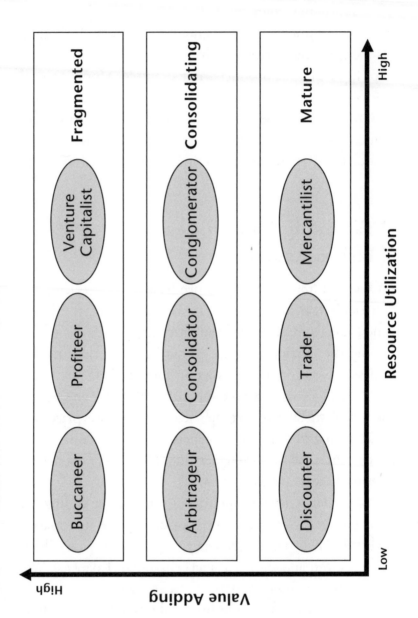

In fact, enterprises should recruit leaders with the intrinsically profitable financial missions, providing that those leaders fit with each enterprise's particular stage of market evolution. In the consolidating phase, for example, an enterprise should hire an Arbitrageur, the one leader with an intrinsically profitable outcome.

Too often, however, enterprises in any type of market hire a Conglomerator or a Consolidator. And, of course, these leaders are unlikely to tell the enterprise that they are not suitable. For one thing, such leaders are simply unaware that they are unsuitable. For another, they sense that the enterprise feels as comfortable with them as they are with the company. Both these leaders and these enterprises may be perfectly sincere, but they are also perfectly misguided. Both have failed to understand that what feels most natural is precisely what they do not need and should stay away from.

Much of the selection of leaders rests on this fundamental misperception by both sides, the leader and the enterprise, of what they need. Most of the failures are due to boards and enterprises recruiting people in their own image who will be bad for them. Unless and until enterprises address the issue of financial signature and financial mission, they will continue to make these errors.

Financial Mission and Industry Type

Industries differ in the level of resources they use. Some industries use resources very heavily, while others use them comparatively lightly.

Our research shows that a leader's financial signature will guide him to those industries that most suit his resource utilization style. This is hardly surprising. For example, a leader with a style of high resource utilization will have some level of discomfort working in an industry where more parsimony is called for. Likewise, a leader who has a low resource utilization style will perceive industries with characteristically high resource utilization as wasteful.

Leaders with high resource utilization styles will gravitate to industries like transportation, defense, technology, communications, construction, and, of course, manufacturing. Industries that require a medium level of investment include consulting, distribution, wholesale and retailing, real estate, finance, publishing, media and healthcare. Industries that require low levels of resource utilization include all of the service industries, including personal care, health practices, temporary help, recruitment, law, accounting, and medicine. The groupings of resource utilization style by market are shown in Figure 12.2. Enterprises recruiting a leader tend to choose those who exhibit a particular predisposition for a particular resource utilization style that characterizes that industry.

A good example of a leader who has stuck to his signature is Jim Kilts, CEO of Gillette and erstwhile CEO of such enterprises as Nabisco and Kraft. These are all manufacturing enterprises in the areas of packaged goods and are high-investment industries.

Kilts is an Arbitrageur. But his Arbitrageur valuation trajectory is that of the High Plateau. Indeed, he has

FIGURE 12.2 Financial mission and industry type.

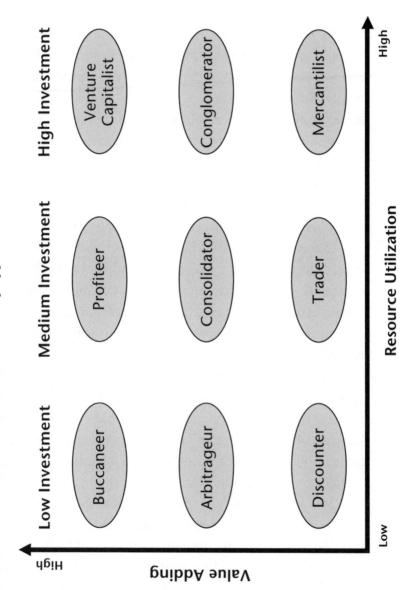

explicitly told analysts that Gillette's high rates of growth are over.[2]

By sticking to the financial mission that he knows best and staying with the same type of industry, Kilts has been successful for all of his enterprises in terms of their profitability and valuation. Kilts is well aware that his own financial mission will result in a fixed market value, and he is not ashamed to make this public so as to set realistic expectations.

But now our model raises another problem in leadership selection: all of the Surplus styles are best suited to low- and medium-investment industries.

In low-investment industries, which include the services, leaders are relatively easy to find. Both the Buccaneer and the Arbitrageur are most suited to the low-investment industries. Only one of the three financial missions, the Discounter, is not intrinsically profitable in this type of industry.

At the medium level of investment, things get a bit harder. In this type of industry, only one of the three financial missions is intrinsically profitable—the Profiteer. Another of the three, the Trader, is intrinsically unprofitable, and the third, namely the Consolidator, is in between.

The major difficulty comes within industries that require a high level of resource utilization. In these industries, no leaders are intrinsically profitable. The Mercantilist and the Conglomerator are both intrinsically unprofitable, while the Venture Capitalist can go either way. Thus, for an enterprise in a high resource utilization industry, a profitable choice does not naturally exist. This conundrum is evident in the airlines and in a company like Boeing or its highly subsidized competitor, Airbus.

An enterprise and its board are always going to have a difficult time selecting a leader who will consistently achieve profits in a high resource utilization industry *unless* they are aware of the concept of financial signature and adjust their leader selection accordingly. In the case of Kilts, for example, the boards that have hired him have consciously selected a leader with a financial mission that is different from the one that their industry culturally prefers.

Of course, many enterprises in high resource utilization industries are profitable— or, at least, seem to be. This profitability partially arises through trial and error. Favorable markets, such as those for defense goods in wartime, also play a part, leading to profits whether the leader is a Mercantilist or Conglomerator. Profitability may also be due in part to shrewd selection by boards and enterprises, which allows leaders to adjust to their financial mission and to correct it.

This last scenario, the shrewd selection, is probably more the exception than the rule. In most cases, an enterprise will select its leader by trial and error. When the markets are favorable, a leader's success will be ascribed to good leadership and good selection rather than to plain good luck. In such cases, the leader will be retained until the market returns to normal and his intrinsically unprofitable financial mission becomes apparent over the longer term.

An enterprise may choose a leader with a propensity for high resource utilization because he seems to fit rather than because it has comprehensively evaluated how likely his financial traits will lead to a profitable outcome. And the leader selects a particular enterprise simply because he feels comfortable with its operating policies.

The fit between enterprise and leader that so often seems natural and logical for both may in fact be a problem for both. The groupings of investment style and financial mission that belong together are shown in Figure 12.2.

Financial Mission and Enterprise Strategy: An Example

The consulting industry spans three levels of resource utilization, from very high-end consultants to low-end consultants, or "body shops." On the value-adding side, it also covers all three levels, from low value adding in the body shops to high value adding with the high-end consultants.

At the high end of the consulting industry are the McKinseys of the world. These companies employ people with high value-adding styles—usually highly analytical and highly educated corporate types. These consultants "rent out" on a fixed-price basis, resulting in relatively high gross margins. Their resource utilization is moderate because they are not developing products or services with high levels of development investment required, but neither are they low. Thus, these high-level consulting enterprises have a Profiteer financial signature, which is associated with a Gently Rising Tide valuation trajectory.

There are relatively few consulting enterprises at the level of McKinsey in the world. Further down the value-added chain, the number of enterprises increases. The major consulting enterprises, such as Accenture, have a lower value-adding propensity but still a medium level of resource utilization. This results in a Consolidator financial culture, which is associated with a Steady State valuation trajectory.

At the low end of the consulting chain are the body shop–type consultants who rent out on a time-and-materials basis to whoever wants to hire them. Gross margins in these enterprises are typically low, and expenses have to be proportionately low as well. Their financial signature is that of the Discounter, and their typical valuation trajectory is the Brown Dwarf.

Anyone who has worked on both sides of this industry will attest that the financial signature of their respective leaders is totally different. Executives with low value-adding signatures cannot work in the high-end side, and vice versa; they simply require different financial signatures.

In the consulting industry, differences among financial styles are, in fact, fairly well understood. The incompatibility of leaders from different segments of the industry is usually ascribed to the differences in culture between these types of organizations. But, in fact, this difference can be more accurately ascribed to the organization's financial culture.

The frequent conflict between auditors and consultants in the erstwhile large audit companies was actually a reflection of different financial signatures and missions. Auditors are usually Discounters, low value adding and low resource utilization. Consultants range from being medium to high value adding and medium to high resource utilization—Arbitrageurs, Consolidators, and Conglomerators, with the odd Profiteer thrown in for good measure. The difference between auditors and consultants resulted in cultural clashes in most of the large combined consulting/auditing companies. Most famously, this led to the split that resulted in the creation of Accenture out of the old Arthur Andersen.

The consulting industry is a microcosm of all the industries. Sometimes, the cultural conflicts caused by the disparate financial signatures in an organization can destroy an enterprise. And leaders with different financial signatures can rarely cross industry boundaries without causing problems for the enterprises they lead.

Market Positioning and Financial Mission

Frequently, an enterprise or its board decides to change its market positioning to improve its competitiveness. If the enterprise decides to move "upmarket," it wishes to increase its margins and its profit potential. If it moves "down-market," its aim is to increase its sales and reduce its overhead per unit of output.

Such strategies may make a lot of sense from the perspective of economic theory. But such changes in market positioning are notoriously difficult to effect, and, typically, they fail. If they do not, they take much longer than anyone ever thought. And usually there are major pockets of resistance that forever doom the repositioning to be suboptimal.

These repositioning efforts rarely take into account the financial traits of the leader. Market repositioning is crucially dependent on the financial mission of the leader. If the financial mission is not consistent with the leader's financial mission, it will almost certainly fail. This is the reason so many repositioning projects, no matter how logical in theory, do not succeed.

For market repositioning to succeed, the enterprise and its board should first understand the financial mission of the leader. After all, few leaders have the maturity and open-mindedness to admit that a planned market repositioning cannot be achieved successfully unless another leader is found. And few boards are prepared to raise the issue of the leader's suitability for the repositioning, even if they suspect that there is an issue.

For example, the architect of the disastrous acquisition of NCR by AT&T was Robert Allen, the chair of AT&T. Allen was a veteran of AT&T. We can surmise that his financial mission was that of the Conglomerator—medium value adding and high resource utilization. But NCR needed someone with a high value-adding financial mission and medium resource utilization—a Profiteer. Allen was unable to fit in with the financial culture required of him on the NCR side, namely high value adding. At the time of the acquisition, there were many doubts. But his board was certainly not going to relay to him that the acquisition would only make sense with a different chair.

Market positioning is strategy. While such strategies can be very clever, they usually fail unless the leadership's financial signature supports the strategy. This discrepancy is why most such strategies fail.

Notes

1 J. Thottam, "Bob the Builder," *Time*, June 21, 2004, 56.

2 K. Brooker, "Gillette: Jim Kilts is an Old-School Curmudgeon. Nothing Could Be Better for Gillette," fortune.com, May 16, 2004, 2.

How Financial Mission Drives Business Strategy

This chapter demonstrated that:

- Financial mission drives particular leaders to lead enterprises at different phases of market evolution.

- Enterprises prefer leaders whose financial mission corresponds to their own financial culture.

- However, the convergent preference of each side is often not the best choice for either one.

- Financial mission predisposes leaders to prefer leading enterprises in certain types of industries.

- Enterprises prefer leaders with an apparently congruent financial mission.

- What each side believes to be a good fit may often actually be bad. Companies usually need leaders with a Surplus style, and they are not easy to find.

- Efforts by enterprises to change their market positioning are often doomed to failure because their current leader does not possess the correct financial mission to do this successfully.

- The repositioning is likely to be successful only if the company takes the leader's financial mission into account.

Top Two Takeaways

▶ When considering a job, make sure your financial mission fits the type of market in which the enterprise participates.

▶ If you are involved in a repositioning for your enterprise, make sure your financial mission is appropriate for it.

SELF-DEVELOPMENT EXERCISE

What is your financial mission?

_____

_____

_____

_____

_____

_____

What type of market does your enterprise participate in?

- Fragmented
- Consolidating
- Mature

Is your financial mission consistent with this market?

_____

_____

_____

_____

_____

_____

If not, what actions could you take to transition to another financial mission?

_____

_____

_____

_____

_____

_____

What type of industry does your enterprise participate in?

- Heavy investment
- Medium investment
- Services

Is your financial mission consistent with this type of industry?

_____

_____

_____

_____

_____

_____

If not, what actions could you take to transition to another financial mission?

_____

_____

_____

_____

_____

_____

_____

_____

_____

_____

_____

_____

_____

_____

_____

_____

_____

LEADERSHIP AND
MARKET VALUE

A Team's
Financial Mission

The study of top management teams (TMT) has traditionally focused on the issue of the personality types of its members, how these types interact, and the internal functioning of the team.

We take a different tack. Our concern is not the interpersonal dynamics of a TMT. Nor is it how well its members function together, although to some extent we can never get away from that topic. Rather, our concern is how a team affects the financial performance and market value of the organization it leads.

In many organizations, particularly smaller ones, the individual leader is the single most important factor in the enterprise's outcome and market value. In larger organizations, this may or may not be the case. Where there is a powerful, even charismatic, leader, the leader may still be the most important factor. We have only to look at individuals such as Citigroup's Sandy Weill or Sunbeam's Al Dunlap to see that.

In many other organizations, the TMT is more important than a single leader, although the team may include the leader. Understanding the TMT's financial mission is important to understanding the organization's valuation trajectory.

Types of Top Management Teams

Traditionally, a TMT is defined as the leader and the core group of managers under him. In a large company, this includes corporate managers and possibly the top P&L managers reporting to them. Understanding the financial missions of these executives would doubtless give us a very good handle on what the outcome and valuation trajectory of the organization might be.

But this is a very restrictive definition. A TMT can also consist of the CEO and the board. After all, these are, at least in theory, the representatives of the shareholders and the key decision makers.

But why stop there? How about management teams under the leader? For example, the division president and his top lieutenants could qualify as a TMT, particularly if they manage the most important division of a company. Or the team under a vice president may be particularly important in driving the outcome and valuation trajectory of a company, especially if it is in the sales or product development area. And what about ad hoc or transitional teams put together for a particular purpose, such as developing and launching a new product, turning a particular division around, or reviewing a failing product? All of these are examples of internal teams, which are not necessarily at the top levels of management but may turn out to be important drivers of the organization's outcome and market value. Even cross-company teams, such as an organization and its suppliers, can have an effect on the organization's outcome.

The organization needs to understand the composition of all such teams from the viewpoint of its composite financial mission. It can then better understand its chances of success and the team's effect on the company's overall outcome and market value.

Partnerships as Teams

Partnerships are also teams, although they are generally comprised of only two or three people. The difference is that they usually have a formal legal basis.

Partnerships are smaller in comparison to the composition of most teams. They also offer a great way to launch the study of TMTs. Once we understand partnerships and the outcome of the financial missions that comprise them, we can move on to bigger and more complex TMTs.

We hear far less about the duos, and occasionally the trios, that form and run a company. Yet many enterprises manage to start and succeed primarily because they were a partnership at the beginning. Many of the most famous enterprises were initially formed as partnerships, including Procter and Gamble, Price Waterhouse (now Price-waterhouseCoopers), Hewlett-Packard, and many others whose names reflect their original founders.

For every Ben and Jerry, however, there are scores of other partnerships that go unrecognized. Warren Buffett has had a partner, Charles Munger, in Berkshire Hathaway since its early days. Oracle was formed as a partnership of three people—Larry Ellison, Bob Miner, and Edward Oates. The famous Ken Olsen of Digital Equipment Corporation formed the company with a partner, Harlan Anderson. And for most of his life, George Eastman of Eastman Kodak had a partner, Henry Strong.

In our database of sixty-seven famous public-company CEOs, there are thirteen partnerships representing twenty-six of the CEOs. In our database of 127 CEOs with whom we have been personally involved, fifteen partnerships comprise a total of 31 CEOs. Partnerships are a lot more common than might at first be imagined.

Numerous enterprises formed as partnerships end up with just one surviving partner. Yet the formation of the company was dependent on there being two, occasionally three, people who pooled their talents and their financial missions.

What is the relationship between the multiple financial signatures in a partnership? How is this relationship related to the company's valuation trajectory? Do different financial signatures perform better in a partnership? These questions can provide a new perspective on the financial performance of individual business leaders. Partnership analysis allows us to explore the fundamentals of team leadership.

Four Types of Partnering Relationships

A partnership may be composed of partners who all have intrinsically profitable financial missions or who all have intrinsically unprofitable financial missions. It may be comprised of missions that can easily go either way. Or it may have a composite of all of the above.

As shown in Figure 13.1, there are four basic types of partnerships, defined according to the partners' financial signatures:

1. Surplus partnerships
2. Deficit partnerships
3. Puzzler partnerships
4. Conflicted partnerships

Although it may appear from Figure 13.1 that a partnership of any combination of missions from one style could be successful, that is not necessarily the case. It all depends on the composition of the types and how similar they are. Let's look at each of these types of partnerships more closely.

Surplus Partnerships

Surplus partnerships are those which comprise only Surplus types of financial missions. They may all be of the same Surplus type, such as all Buccaneers. Or they may comprise different Surplus types. The first group implies a powerful Surplus team. The latter case implies a Surplus approach, but one split by disagreements as to

FIGURE 13.1 Financial mission and the top management team.

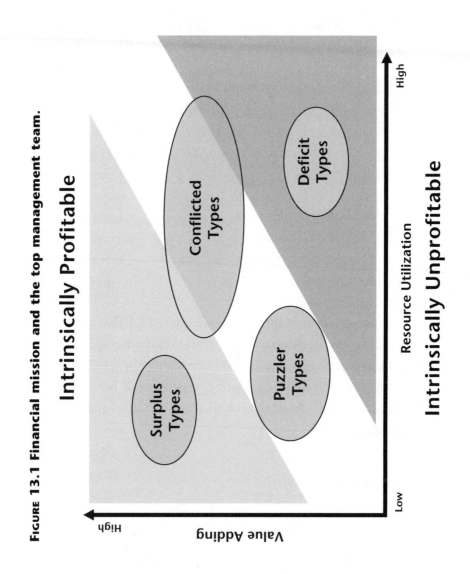

the precise way to achieve earnings and create company value.

Berkshire Hathaway is an example of a Surplus partnership. Warren Buffet and Charles Munger have always been seen as being very similar. The famous Ben Graham, who knew them both, remarked on how strongly alike they were.[1] In fact, Buffett and Munger are both Arbitrageurs, with a medium value-adding propensity. Both are legendary for taking very carefully calculated risks in enterprises that are not breakthrough, but create just enough value to get them out of trouble. They avoid enterprises that take them into any area of value adding that spells danger and runaway costs, and they are quintessentially averse to anything but the lowest levels of resource utilization. As a Surplus partnership, Berkshire Hathaway has been very successful.

Another intriguing example of a Surplus partnership is John Reed and Sandy Weill while they were still co-CEOs at Citibank. This partnership later collapsed, and Weill was the sole survivor.

Both Weill and Reed had high–value-added styles. But they differed markedly in resource utilization. Weill was very low resource utilization; Reed was at a medium or even a high level. At best, Reed was a Profiteer, but more likely he was on the edge between Profiteer and Venture Capitalist. He had had a long career with Citibank and was inured to their high-spending financial culture. Weill, of course, was the reverse. Although both were intrinsically profitable, Reed was slightly so and Weill very much so.

Naturally, this led to conflicts very early on. Leaders with different financial missions have different models for creating value. So it was with Reed and Weill, even though they both had Surplus financial styles. One of them had to go.

Surplus partnerships are not very common. In our CEO database, only 13 percent are Surplus partnerships. This does not mean numerous other examples do not exist. However, the evidence suggests that they are inherently uncommon, in part because there are so few leaders with a Surplus financial style.

Enterprises can increase their chances of success by selecting leaders who do possess such a mission. However, they may not be good at leader selection, or they may have no useful model, which leads to them having a random probability of selecting the right leader. In these cases, which probably account for the majority of enterprises, they will probably end up selecting leaders with Deficit styles.

Deficit Partnerships

Deficit partnerships comprise only Deficit financial styles, but they can have combinations of the three constituents: Trader, Mercantilist, and Conglomerator.

Obviously, if the partners are all of the same Deficit type, there is a powerful tendency to generate losses. If they are in different Deficit categories, this tendency will be magnified. Not only are they intrinsically money-losers over the long term, but they also differ on the ways in which to generate losses.

These partnerships do not last very long because they lose money so quickly they go out of existence. As a result, there are not many of this particular type in our CEO databases, but there is one case study worth noting.

A public company sold and delivered a certain type of business service. Its CEO is Case 12, and its chief financial officer is Case 13. Although in title these two had a traditional reporting relationship, in practice they were essentially partners, though not in a strictly legal sense. But they consulted each other on everything and in every way acted as partners.

Case 12 had come from the industry and knew the business well, but he had come from a large company in a senior functional management position. He had never run a company before. Case 13 had been an accountant and had never run a company before, either. Both had low value-adding propensities. Case 12 had high resource utilization tendencies, Case 13 medium. Case 12 was a Mercantilist, while Case 13 was a Trader.

With both leaders possessing Deficit financial styles, the company lost money—lots of it. These two leaders were never able to craft a model to make earnings because they were simply incapable of doing so.

In addition, the two partners had significant disagreements regarding how to create value. Case 12 felt that the company could best create value by spending more, so they invested heavily in new equipment. Case 13 did not really agree with this, although he went along.

As both leaders had power in the company, they each executed their own preferred strategies. This resulted in employee and customer confusion and even greater losses.

Eventually, the company went bankrupt and had to be liquidated.

Many leaders get to their position by being visionary without necessarily being financially canny. These are the Venture Capitalists. Partnerships with both a Venture Capitalist and a Deficit type often end up as de facto Deficit partnerships. This also happens when the Deficit type is the dominant partner. The partnership sinks to the financial mission of the lowest common denominator because it creates the least conflict between them. Few such enterprises have a happy ending.

Puzzler Partnerships

Puzzlers are the most intriguing of our partnership types, as we never really know what the outcome of their leadership will be. Their value-adding and resource utilization tendencies have similar strengths, so there is no intrinsic surplus or deficit. It is up to the roll of the dice.

Puzzler partnerships exist between the three middle financial styles, the Discounter, the Venture Capitalist, and the Consolidator. In our database, Puzzler partnerships are by far the most common type.

The most common Puzzler partnerships in our database are those between two Venture Capitalists. Their financial mission emphasizes breakthroughs and world-changing strategies. It also incorporates the high investments, usually excessive in a purely financial sense, needed to achieve them. One of the best examples of a Puzzler partnership in recent years is the two founders of Yahoo, Jerry Yang and David Filo.

On the surface, Yang and Filo look more different than they actually are. Both have high value-adding tendencies, which attracted them to each other while they were still students at Stanford. But both are also high resource utilization and execution oriented but not financially focused.

Yang and Filo each have a Venture Capitalist financial mission. As a result, they ran into early losses. Indeed, this was why Tim Koogle was hired as CEO.[2] Their Puzzler partnership could only be corrected with the addition of another person who had a different, Surplus financial mission.

Koogle seemed to fit the bill. He was certainly high value adding, and he was an experienced manager. But Koogle had a quasi-Venture Capitalist and quasi-Profiteer financial mission, which was not different enough from that of the two founding partners to have a positive effect on market value. Yahoo did not achieve the financial results it needed, and the board opted for yet another change.

The change was to Terry Semel, who is clearly different from Yang and Filo. If anything, he has an Arbitrageur financial mission that is very different from the founders'. It is a Surplus style, but it is associated with a High Plateau valuation trajectory, which is, arguably, exactly what Yahoo's valuation direction has become on his watch.

Puzzler partnerships between two Discounters are also relatively common. These partnerships form because the partners realize that they have very similar ways of creating value.

Keep in mind that when two or more leaders enter into a partnership, they only have their intuition as to what financial mission the other partner actually represents. More likely, each leader feels that the other person is somewhat similar to himself and that together they would be better as a team than working individually.

Conflicted Partnerships

Conflicted partnerships are the most complex of all because they mix Deficit, Surplus, and Puzzler types. Because of this mix of financial missions, we cannot know in advance what the financial effect will be. We call these partnerships Conflicted because they incorporate an inherent conflict. It is not just that they contain types that have different ways of creating value. They also have intrinsically different financial styles.

For a Deficit leader, a Puzzler often appears to be a route to success. The Deficit partner recognizes that a Puzzler has a chance to make it, possibly in a significant way. And a Puzzler is certainly better than another Deficit partner. Meanwhile, a Puzzler leader may team up with a Deficit type for a variety of reasons. He may lack experience and not see the warning signs, or the Deficit partner may be dominant or persuasive.

A Surplus type has a different thought process in teaming with a Puzzler. Wishful thinking on the part of the Surplus leader may make the Puzzler appear to be a Surplus leader—a comrade-in-arms. In this partnership, the Puzzler sees the Surplus type for what he is, a probable route to success—certainly, one who can do better than he can.

To an Arbitrageur, a Consolidator may appear to have big investment ideas that he would not dare try on his own. And to the Consolidator in this partnership, the Arbitrageur looks like a sure route to regular cash flow, which he knows privately he can never achieve on his own. A Deficit or a Surplus partnership may have different ways of creating value but the same underlying financial style. Members of a Conflicted partnership do not even have the same financial style to keep them together. As a result, Conflicted partnerships often end up splitting up; they are simply too incompatible and unstable to sustain a long-term relationship.

A good example of a Conflicted partnership is that between Ken Olsen and Harlan Anderson of Digital Equipment Corporation. In many ways, these two men were very similar. Both had a computer engineering background.[3] They had virtually no business experience or smarts, nor did they have any interest or expertise in financial matters.[4]

They differed sharply in their financial mission, however. Olsen was a Profiteer, Anderson a Venture Capitalist. Their similar value-adding tendencies were the glue that attracted them to each other in the first place, but their resource utilization styles were very different.

Anderson believed that high resource utilization was necessary to stay ahead of the pack. For Olsen, profits were the main goal. The conflicts between them became ever more discordant on this point. After many years, Anderson was forced out of DEC by Olsen, as Olsen's strategies were leading to DEC's profits and market value.

The largest group of Conflicted partners occurs between Surplus types and Puzzlers. A good example is

Bill Gates and Paul Allen, the cofounders of Microsoft. Both had high value-adding tendencies, which brought them together in the first place. Allen in particular preferred taking major risks. Some of these risks have been successful, such as America Online and DreamWorks. Many more were unsuccessful.[5] Thus, although Gates and Allen were both essentially risk-takers, Allen was much more so.

Gates had low resource utilization levels, while Allen had a propensity for high resource utilization. Gates was always highly oriented to the numbers; Allen was not. Gates was an intuitive businessman. Allen was not; he viewed ideas first and foremost, and business last.[6] Gates was a Buccaneer, Allen a Venture Capitalist. Such a situation could not last, as each had radically different ideas on how to create value. Although Allen ostensibly left Microsoft due to an illness, it was clear that this partnership could not last.

Contrast this with the de facto partnership between Bill Gates and Steve Ballmer, CEO after Allen. They are both Buccaneers, which has worked very well for a long time.

In our databases, it is unusual to find Conflicted partnerships from the *opposite* sides of the model. For example, although they exist, it is unusual to find a Profiteer, say, with a Mercantilist or a Trader with a Buccaneer. It appears that such prospective partners quickly work out that their financial missions are so unalike that the arrangement would never work. Where such partnerships exist, it is usually between younger partners who have less business experience or between partners who are thrown together for reasons beyond their control, such as a merger.

It would be very useful to know, in advance, whether a partnership is in the Conflicted category. For example, an investor would love to know whether the two cofounders of a venture have a Conflicted partnership or otherwise. The same holds for professional partnerships, such as doctors and lawyers.

Going beyond the usual discussions regarding personal compatibility in a partnership to assess the compatability of financial missions helps us to determine whether the partnership can ever work and create enduring financial value.

Partnerships and Financial Mission

In the traditional management and leadership theory, observers stress that what makes a team great is diversity. According to this approach, management and leadership teams should be balanced. Then leaders will be able to compensate for their shortcomings through the competencies that other team members possess.

In practice, however, at least as far as financial signature is concerned, the opposite is true. The best teams are homogeneous in their financial missions. This homogeneity avoids the conflict of how value will be created.

Even on Surplus-style teams, it pays to have the same financial mission. If all team members are on the Surplus side but have different missions, the chance of achieving a good outcome declines. And, of course, there is no obvious reason to pair a Surplus leader with a Deficit leader. The only exception would be to achieve a highly specific short-term goal, which a leader with a particular Deficit mission could help achieve.

With this one Surplus/Deficit exception, financial mission diversity will not work. Moreover, over the longer haul, teams would even want to avoid the most common types, the Puzzlers. They could work out well, but just as easily they could help the team lose its shirt. Far better to find a Surplus type right off the bat and save the aggravation.

Teams and Financial Mission

By analyzing partnerships, we have actually been conducting a stealth analysis on teams. In this process, we identified four types of partnerships. By extension, we can infer that these are also four types of teams. These are the Surplus, Deficit, Puzzler, and Conflicted teams. These teams will have exactly the same characteristics as the partnerships outlined above.

• **Surplus teams** comprise only members with an intrinsically profitable financial mission. They can include one or more missions. If there is more than one type, however, they will have a higher potential for disagreement and failure, Surplus styles notwithstanding.
• **Deficit teams** include only members with a Deficit style. They, too, can comprise one or more missions, which will almost certainly create losses over the

longer term. If more than one mission is involved, there will be a higher potential for disagreement, which will lead to even greater losses. This is our nightmare vision of a team.

• **Puzzler teams** are composed of financial styles that can have either a positive or negative market value outcome. Even if the members are all of the same mission, this will not change the basic equation. But if they are of more than one type, their potential to swing to a good outcome is reduced because of the different Puzzler models for creating value.

• **Conflicted teams** include members from Surplus, Deficit, and/or Puzzler types. These usually have significant problems and will split up relatively quickly. In general, the more missions involved, the worse the outcome. Knowing who is dominant in the team helps predict the likely outcome. Failing that, we would avoid these types or do some fundamental reengineering.

The concept of the financial mission provides us with a totally new tool for analyzing the effect of teams on the market value of the organization they lead.

Designer Teams for Enterprise Valuation

In this book, we have constantly emphasized that we should view leadership only in terms of its outcome. For us, market value is outcome. By the same token, we should assess teams in the same way.

The aim of enterprises should be to set up teams that have as their mission the achievement of particular and specific valuation trajectories. These teams should be custom designed to have this effect.

Different teams will lead to different valuation trajectories. Profiteer teams will lead to a Gently Rising Tide valuation trajectory, for example, and Buccaneer teams will lead to a Fast-Rising Tide trajectory. We would not normally mix our teams without specific goals in mind. Then we would set up truly designer teams to match the various financial missions of the team members to the particular financial goals we have set for the team.

The concept of the financial mission recognizes that leadership is for a purpose—market value creation. Teams that lead are there for the same purpose, to increase company value.

Notes

1 J. Lowe, *Damn Right: Behind the Scenes with Berkshire Hathaway Billionaire Charlie Munger*, New York: John Wiley, 2000, 2.

2 K. Angel, *Inside Yahoo: Reinvention and the Road Ahead*, New York: John Wiley, 2002, 39–41.

3 G. Rifkin and G. Harrar, *The Ultimate Entrepreneur: The Story of Ken Olsen and Digital Equipment Corporation*, Chicago, Contemporary Books, 1988, 9.

4 Ibid., 29, 53.

5 L. Rich, *The Accidental Zillionaire: Demystifying Paul Allen*, Hoboken, NJ: John Wiley, 2003, 188.

6 Ibid., 118.

A Team's Financial Mission

This chapter demonstrated that:

▶ Teams are an important leadership issue.

▶ Partnerships are an important form of a team.

▶ We can analyze teams using partnerships as a starting point.

▶ The four types of both partnerships and teams are the Surplus, Deficit, Puzzler, and Conflicted types, each of which has a characteristic impact on company outcome and market value.

▶ Teams need to be designed to meet certain predefined objectives.

▶ The only way to assess the value of a team is by its ultimate effect on the valuation trajectory of an organization.

Top Two Takeaways

▶ Make sure that the members of any team you are involved in have financial missions that are as close as possible to yours.

▶ When seeking a promotion, make sure that your new boss and the managers under him or her have much the same financial mission as you.

SELF-DEVELOPMENT EXERCISE

If you lead a team in your enterprise or if you are a team member, note the financial missions of the other team members.

1. _____

2. _____

3. _____

4. _____

5. _____

How closely aligned are these financial missions?

_____

_____

_____

_____

_____

_____

_____

_____

If they are closely aligned, what is the likely valuation trajectory of the team?

_____

_____

_____

_____

_____

_____

If they are not closely aligned, what actions can you take to achieve a closer alignment?

_____

_____

_____

_____

_____

_____

CHAPTER 14

Uncovering
a Leader's
Financial Signature

There are three major reasons to determine a leader's financial signature. The first is that you want to support the leader of your enterprise. The second is that you are interested in joining the leader's enterprise as an employee, partner, team member, or investor. And the third is that you want to do business with the leader's company.

Supporting the Leader

Not all business leaders are instant successes; in fact, very few are. More typically, a leader will have problems early on in running a business. Sometimes these problems lead to the leader's ultimate failure. Whatever the outcome, while the leader struggles, the enterprise also struggles, along with its many constituents.

No one wants a leader to fail. If she fails, so does everyone, including the community. Everyone has a vested interest in helping our leaders succeed. And many people—investors, stockholders, bankers, suppliers, customers, employees, and colleagues—want to support their leaders in practical and useful ways.

To help a leader, you have to understand more about her. Knowing her financial mission is a vital first step. Once you understand the leader's financial mission, you will understand much more about why there are problems. You start to comprehend what types of support she needs and how you can participate in these mechanisms.

Our research shows that there are actually two components of leadership. One is leadership, the other is followership. Followership is a noble, but overlooked, goal of leadership. By developing good followers who understand and support them, leaders build better organizations and institutions.

The function of a leadership model is to provide practical guidance to both leaders *and* followers, to leaders so that they can better lead, and to followers so that they can better support. The financial mission provides this model. Instead of focusing on the leader and her personal issues, it focuses on the effect of the leader on the market value of the enterprise.

Joining the Leader's Enterprise

Once you know the leader's financial mission, you can understand the possible market value outcomes for the enterprise.

Knowing the leader's financial mission will tell you:

- Whether the leader's financial mission is intrinsically profitable
- Whether your financial mission is aligned with his and his team's
- The effect of the leader's financial mission on the enterprise's sales, products, and operations
- Whether the leader has the correct financial mission for the market structure the enterprise participates in
- Whether the leader's financial mission, the enterprise's stage of evolution, and the type of product or service it sells match
- The quality of the market value that will result from this leader's work
- The potential valuation trajectory of the enterprise

As a prospective employee, partner, team member, or investor, this is vital and useful information. It will give you some insights into your prospects and future with the enterprise.

Doing Business with the Leader

The ultimate form of selling is to a business leader, no matter what his level, because he has the power to make a decision on the spot. But there are no courses that teach us specifically how to sell to business leaders or top executives. We believe, however, that you can significantly increase your chances of selling to top executives by understanding their financial mission.

Problems in Uncovering the Business Leader's Financial Signature

Business leaders, like most of us, are sensitive about revealing their inner selves. They may feel uncomfortable about revealing personal information about their financial habits, skills, and performance and, thus, be reluctant to share information. Some leaders may be insecure about their ability to perform. Some may be concerned that discussing their financial style will uncover some of their secret or proprietary strategies. Others may think that it is a waste of time.

To discover a leader's financial signature, you will need to successfully address two common problems. One is that the leader is not aware of her financial signature, the other is that she is unwilling to reveal her financial signature, even though she knows what it is.

Problem 1: The Leader Is Unaware of His or Her Financial Signature

Asking a leader about his financial signature will generally prove fruitless because very few know what it is. Our work with clients often begins with this very assignment;

future engagements frequently hinge on recognizing a leader's financial style.

In working with a leader, we ask him to complete a formal assessment. But we do not want to rely totally on the assessment. Most assessments are pretty accurate, but there are exceptions. Some leaders are tired when they complete it. Others try to present themselves in the best light. The odd one may try to manipulate its outcome. Or the assessment may just not capture them very well.

To supplement the assessment and improve its accuracy, we also ask the leader directly. We usually present the financial signature model. Even then, both the business leader and the reviewer may not recognize where the client is on one or both of the scales.

Take one of our clients, Case 14, the CEO of a small enterprise. Case 14 had attended one of our seminars and was fascinated by the link between financial signature and enterprise outcome.

However, after we began working together and identified his financial signature, Case 14 started to shift the discussion away from financial signature, as it was difficult for him. He readily saw the lessons pertaining to him and quickly adopted our recommendations concerning changes to managing the enterprise. But he much preferred talking about these issues rather than his own financial signature.

Case 14 is typical. Many leaders understand intuitively the importance of their financial signature and can accept changing the way they do things. But discussing their profile in detail can be difficult because such a direct approach in many ways resembles therapy. And like therapy, it involves self-analysis, which is potentially painful when leaders recognize that their self-image may not reflect reality. Yet to perform better, they have to accept reality.

For the vast majority of readers of this book, there will be no formal assessment. In most cases, you will have no access whatsoever to the leader. Instead, you can use field-discovery techniques, such as reviewing publicly available information and interviewing personal contacts, to paint a picture of the leader's financial signature.

Problem 2: The Leader Is Unwilling to Reveal His or Her Financial Signature

A leader may be self-aware enough to have an intuitive feel for her financial signature and mission. This happens with many experienced leaders. But she may not wish to expose it for social, political, business, or emotional reasons.

Take Case 15, the CEO of a small computer company. Case 15 was an extrovert. He was very good at getting his name out and had been successful in securing financing for his company. But Case 15 was a Mercantilist, something he did not want to expose because he felt that this could be perceived as a negative to his investors.

Fortunately, there is an answer for the problem of leaders who attempt to disguise or conceal their financial signature. You can often read it in the financial metrics of their enterprise.

Principles of Discovery

A formal instrument for assessing the financial signature of a business leader can be completed through the Perth Leadership Institute. Providing the leader will consent to complete it, you are in business.

In many instances, however, you will be unable to convince a leader to complete it. Or you may simply never have direct contact with him. In those instances, you can use some alternative approaches to discovering his financial signature.

Actions, Not Words

There are numerous traps in discovering financial signature. Words may not count for much. As an analyst of financial signature, you must ensure that you make your judgments based on actions, not on words. This is akin to how you judge a politician: No matter what she says, the gold standard is what she does. The same holds true for the business leader.

You must find information sources that are independent, or to some extent at arm's length. This means that an autobiography is not much use to your analysis, unless it is merely used to contrast with other sources. Autobiographies tell you what the business leader believes to be the case or what she would like you to hear. They may tell you about the strategies she implemented and why or give you perspective on her decisions and actions, but autobiographies will not tell you much about the leader's true motives—and certainly not much about her financial signature.

No Wrong Answers

You have probably heard it before: There are no wrong answers. You are what you are. Once you know what you are, you can move forward.

This is a crucial principle. Too often, everyone tries to hide what he or she is. Yet if you do not know where you stand in your financial signature, you will not know how to correct yourself and your financial performance. And if you deceive yourself, you might make the wrong decisions about correcting your leadership approaches. This means, at best, that the market value of the organization you lead will not be optimized as a result. More likely, it will lose money and not create value.

Discovery Techniques

We now turn to the discovery techniques themselves, keeping in mind that there are huge differences between the techniques used for leaders of public companies and for leaders of private enterprises or corporate divisions. Leaders of public companies are, in principle, the easiest to track. Their stock is publicly traded, so there are always people following their actions in some way. Numerous types of formal documents must be publicly filed by public enterprises, and they get more press. Their financial results are publicly available, so you can use them to infer much about their leaders' financial signatures.

The leader of a private enterprise and the manager of a division of a public or private company pose the same issues of discovery. They have no published financials. There are no regularly filed documents in the public domain. Press reports are less common, and cannot be checked back against any financial information. But there are still ways to uncover financial signature for these leaders.

Uncovering the Financial Signature of the Public-Company Leader

Several sources can help you discover the financial signature of the leader of a public company. These include:

- Public filings and financial statements
- Books and biographies
- Media coverage
- Internet discussion groups and chat forums
- Analysts
- Customers and industry partners
- Press releases

Public Filings and Financial Statements

Public filings and financial statements are probably the easiest place to start researching a leader's financial signature.

Background Information. A corporation's proxy statement will contain a biography of its leader, including his previous experience, his educational background, and his age. It can quickly provide you with the professional face of the business leader.

How does knowing a leader's background help you? While there are no absolute rules, there are some trends. People with financial and accounting backgrounds are often frugal, with at least no more than a medium level of resource utilization. Usually, they are low value adding, although, of course, there are always exceptions.

Leaders with sales backgrounds are often high resource utilization. They are used to investing in sales forces, and they work to enrich the customer experience, which often requires high expenditures on promotion. And they tend to be lower on the value-adding component, because they invest in the customer experience rather than in the product or service itself.

Leaders with technical, engineering, or systems backgrounds tend to be lower in the area of resource utilization. They are not generally focused on enriching the customer experience, nor are they oriented to invest in promotion. They also tend to have higher value-adding tendencies.

Public filings also allow you to check how the leader performed in previous positions. A history of losses may be due to a weak product and a poor market, or it may be due to the leader's Deficit financial style, which has not been apparent. Maybe he is a very articulate and persuasive individual who can explain away a history of losses as due to factors other than his financial style—or maybe not.

The proxy statement also provides biographies and backgrounds of the directors and officers of the company. This tells you the types of people the leader gravitates to. You may see a systematic bias in these types of people from which you may be able to infer some components of his financial signature. For example, the directors and officers may overwhelmingly come from sales. If the leader also has a sales background, you might conclude that the company is higher on the resource utilization scale.

Financial Information. Public filings will also provide you with an abundance of information concerning the financial performance of the company. You can find this information in the 10Q and the 10K filings, the quarterly and annual reports. You can use these reports to shed more light on the financial signature of the business leader through the quantitative perspective provided.

The length of time a leader needs to affect the financials will depend on the type of product the company produces and its industry group. Some may take several years to affect the financials, while others take just a few months. This depends on the average development cycle time and the average sales cycle of the company.

As always, beware of accounting strategies and maybe even stratagems. The financials you review may not accurately reflect what is going on in the company. Unusual accounting techniques may be in use, either legitimately or otherwise. Some financial metrics are easier to get at than others, but these may not be as useful as those that are harder to find and interpret.

Expenses. Resource utilization is probably the easier of the two components to assess. We can find this in the profit-and-loss (P&L) statement.

Company expenses are a key metric. See what expenses are as a percentage of revenues, and compare the expense ratio to other enterprises in the same industry using publicly available information.

You can also analyze the components of total expenses—research and development (R&D), sales and marketing, and general and administrative (G&A). Again, check these against other public enterprises to see whether they are above or below average.

If the leader of a company has been at the helm for more than a year and average expenses on these metrics are above average, a judgment as to higher resource utilization may be in order. If so, you would want to check for qualitative indications from other sources, both written and otherwise. The same is true of expenses that are lower than average.

Value Adding. The value-adding component is best viewed using gross margin as the key metric, which can also be found in the P&L statement. Here, too, you need to be careful, as not all enterprises or industries adopt the same accounting basis for gross margin. But you can compare gross margin levels for comparable enterprises that are in the same industry or that offer the same or a similar product or service.

This data is easy to find. But you cannot just compare gross margin levels without using an industry or product as a baseline. In retailing, a gross margin of 25 percent is very high; in software, it is very low. In consulting, it could be low or high, depending on the type of consulting.

Once again, you need to take into account the length of time for the leader's financial signature to have an effect. The higher the value adding, the longer it will take for the leader's financial signature to affect the company's financials. For a high–value-added industry, it could be three years or even more. For a service industry, it could be one year or less.

Books and Biographies

If the company is big enough, you will be able to find detailed information on its leader. It may be big enough that there is a company biography.

Biographies allow you to gain more personal information about the profile subject than purely business-oriented books. And biographies by third parties are probably more objective than autobiographies or sponsored books.

Above all, make sure that the biography is not an "approved" biography. This occurs when the leader has approved the contents in return for giving the author increased access. In many cases, these are just promotional materials for the leader or her company disguised as a book.

Media Coverage

Media coverage, such as newspaper and magazine articles, can be a very good way to uncover a financial signature. True, some of the information may be self-serving. But the reporter may also provide independent observations that shed light on a leader's financial signature.

For example, an article about a business leader that notes his acquisition of expensive things for his own use and aggrandizement may ring a warning bell. It is not just the echo of Tyco and Enron, where there may have been outright malfeasance, as this occurs within the context of many other companies where everything is legal. But the high-expense style tells you that the leader may have a high-expense financial signature. This, in turn, tells us much about the company outcome, such as that expenses may be higher than the average so market value is likely to be lower, other things being equal.

The reporter may interview other people who know the business leader well and who refer to his value-adding style. They may refer to the leader as someone who is inventive, a thinker or a tinkerer, or as someone who does not like getting involved in the details or even the strategy of the product or service that the company sells. These comments can provide useful information about where the leader stands on the value-adding component of the financial signature.

Media coverage also includes television. Your understanding of a leader's financial signature may well be advanced by seeing the leader live, so to speak. Is he defensive or confident? Does he answer the questions as asked, particularly those about expenses or product value and progress? Is he bombastic or evasive? Does he appear reserved or ebullient? What are his spending patterns likely to be, given these traits? When watching such coverage, remember that some people are more telegenic than others. The impression you get may not be very reliable, but television is still another valuable source of information.

Internet Discussion Groups and Chat Forums

Internet forums can be invaluable sources of feedback. Many public enterprises have discussion groups devoted to them on Yahoo and other online services. Many stock sites also have discussion groups about many public enterprises.

If you are lucky, one or more of the participants may be a current or ex-employee who can provide firsthand information on the business leader. Sometimes, disgruntled employees get onto the sites and provide useful information. At the same time, however, be careful because there may well be legal issues involved.

Also, remember that this information may be highly biased. As always, be careful and suitably critical. The sites can be a good source of tidbits and opinions. If you continue to participate in the forums, you may start to see patterns, which you may choose to discuss with other members of the forum.

Remember, though, that these websites need to be treated with care. Often, they are a forum for people who have a bone to pick, with either the company or the leader. They may have members who are trying to push the stock one way or the other using questionable information. You might even encounter employees of competing enterprises who are only too eager to provide disinformation. As with all information on the Web, you need to be suitably critical, careful, and cautious in interpretation.

Analysts

These days, far fewer enterprises have financial analysts assigned to monitor and report on them than used to be the case. But when they do, these analysts can be another source of information on financial signature. Sometimes, this information is too technical to be of interest. If the analyst can comment on the leader's personal style or habits, however, she can provide details that indicate the leader's financial signature.

Sometimes this will be in the context of the figures ("the leader has been spending a lot of resources on his favorite new product idea . . . and earnings seem to have been affected"). On other occasions it may be a one-off impression of the leader as a person ("Joe, the CEO, seems to have an incremental view of product strategy"). Either way, these insights can add to your inventory of information.

A particularly intriguing possibility for finding information is quarterly analysts' calls. These are teleconferences run by the company every quarter, normally addressed by the leader. They are used as a vehicle for the CEO to comment on the company's quarterly results and to answer questions on them. Although the audience typically includes analysts and market-makers, companies have increasingly been opening up these calls to other participants.

If you are lucky enough to be in on one of these calls, you can advance your information gathering in several ways. First, you can listen to the business leader in person, which will, in and of itself, provide you with additional information and insights. Second, and even more useful, you can listen to the business leader being asked questions for which he has not prepared. Lastly, you can ask questions yourself.

If understanding a business leader's financial signature is your aim, you should try to participate in such calls. Naturally, you would need to be a stockholder yourself. But if your aim is to assess the investment you have in the company's stock, you are already one.

Customers and Industry Partners

If the company you are investigating is big enough, you may well be able to locate customers or partners. While the individual you talk to may not have met the leader in question, they may know other people who have.

These days, with the Internet and e-mail, it is quite possible to track down people who have such information just by asking. Even if the company is a smaller one, you may be able to find such people through press releases or through references in the public filings to new or existing customers.

Press Releases

Press releases can be a very revealing source of information about a leader. Do the releases provide more insight concerning why expenses are rising or declining? Do the releases indicate that the company is hyping new products or services that are at best incremental in nature rather than the major breakthroughs they are being presented as? Reading between the lines, is the company under competitive pressure, reflecting a lack of good ideas?

Reading press releases is a bit like interpreting old Soviet propaganda releases. They may often appear boring and devoid of interest, but a closer, more critical reading may tell you a lot. And what is omitted may be more important than what is included.

Press releases can provide you with a lot of information if you are prepared to look critically. Literary analysis may yield more important insights here than financial analysis.

Uncovering the Financial Signature of the Private-Company Leader

There are several reasons for discovering the financial signature of leaders and managers of private enterprises and of divisions of public or private companies. These include:

- You are seeking employment in a private company or in a division or other unit of a public company.
- The leader is seeking funding. You do not know him, but his request has come through a mutual connection.
- The enterprise is seeking a partnership with your company. You want to assess the leader to determine whether his financial signature is consistent with your objectives.

You can use many of the same methods to study the private-enterprise leader as for the public-company leader. Although there are no company filings, there may still be books, articles, and press releases.

In addition to the public sources already covered, there are some other information sources to be used where no such information exists. These sources include:

- Websites
- Interviews
- Employees
- Customer support representatives
- Social networking

Websites

A website is a much more important tool for studying a private enterprise than it is for a public company.

For a private company or for a division of a public company, a website may provide the only public information available. And it may or may not be a rich source. Usually, the website will tell you the name of the leader and give you her background as well as that of the management team and perhaps of board members. It will often provide the names of customers and partners. Frequently, you can also find e-mail addresses of key contact people at the company.

Corporate partners can be particularly useful. Once you know their names, you can check out their websites, too. You can contact them by e-mail or phone to ask for information about the company and the leader you have an interest in.

Interviews

You can use interviews for both types of business leaders. It may be difficult or impossible to obtain an interview with the leader of a large public company but more likely for a small private company or a unit of a public company. It may or may not be in-person, but even a phone interview is still very useful.

Many private enterprises are seeking capital and, to that end, have prepared a business plan or offering memorandum to share with prospective investors. The business plan, if you can get ahold of one, is a useful document for preparing for an interview. The forecasts included in a business plan can give you insights as to the leader's financial signature by showing what he projects in resource utilization and value adding. You can then compare this to industry norms, just as you would a public company.

The focus of the business plan will give you some idea as to what the leader focuses on most. If it is very product oriented, for example, you may infer that his technical background drives much of his decision making and actions and that he may have high value adding in his financial signature. If the focus is more about sales, marketing, and customers, and he has a sales background, the plan may suggest a very high-expense company. If the plan is very heavily financially oriented, that may reflect a company that is low value adding and low resource utilizations. Or maybe it is focused on acquisitions or deal-making.

If the company indeed is seeking capital, you have a ready-made approach for your interview. How much capital is required? What will the investor receive in return? What does the company expect to achieve with this investment? What are the terms of the investment? The answers to these questions will provide you with insights into the financial signature of the business leader. The more you can question the leader, the more you will understand where he may fit on the value-adding and resource utilization scales.

You may be able to arrange an interview with the leader in person. An in-person meeting allows you to conduct a broader-ranging interview, which can help answer many of your questions about his financial signature. You can also keep your eyes peeled for telltale signs of excessive spending or for great value adding.

Remember that even with an interview, third-party information is necessary to make a full determination of a leader's financial signature.

Employees

By far, the best information you can obtain is from employees, who usually know their leader well. They have seen her act in many different types of situations. They are generally at arm's length, so they can be objective.

The best way to contact an employee is through the sales department. You may want to call just to ask for a brochure. You may want to find out more about the product. If you contact the sales department about buying, it would be a rare salesperson who would not call back to talk with you about the product, its competitors, the company, and probably the leader.

Customer Support Representatives

The customer support department is another place to go for information. Generally, the customer support representatives (CSRs) may not be as talkative. You might have to buy the product first. Generally, they will provide information about the product, its performance, and maybe even its competition.

In some cases, CSRs might even talk about their leader. They might also refer you to their boss. Although people are very busy, if someone is genuinely interested in the company, they are prepared to take some time out to discuss it, especially if they are very proud of their product or their company. If they are not prepared to discuss much at all, you may want to find out why. That in itself may tell you something about the financial signature of the company's leader.

Social Networking

It helps enormously to talk with people who have first-hand knowledge of the business leader. If you cannot find any of these people, then technology may come to your rescue. A new type of application is enabling people to network on the Web. You can network to find friends, a job, or like-minded people.

These applications, such as Friendster, Spoke Connect, LinkedIn, and Ryze, allow enterprises to tap the hidden value in the networks of their employees for sales, recruitment, and other corporate purposes. Social networking applications also promise a powerful new means of finding information about a leader's financial signature by enabling you to find people who know them personally, even in the smallest enterprises.

Discovering a Leader's Financial Signature

This chapter demonstrated that:

▶ Reasons to uncover the financial signature of a leader include to support him or her, to obtain a job or even to investigate investment opportunities, and to conduct business with a leader or top executive.

▶ Most business leaders are unaware of their financial signature.

▶ You should rely on actions rather than words in conducting your analysis.

▶ There are particular signals and clues, such as knowing a leader's background, that provide shortcuts to recognizing components of the financial signature.

▶ We need somewhat different techniques to investigate leaders in public and private enterprises.

▶ The financial statements of a public company provide vital information for inferring the financial signature of a business leader.

▶ It is important to try to talk with people, such as employees, suppliers, customers, and partners, who know the leader in question.

▶ A business plan is useful for discovering the financial signature of a leader of a private company.

Top Two Takeaways

▶ Discover your new boss's financial signature before you take a promotion or a new job to make sure that your missions are aligned and that you will not experience unforeseen problems with him or her.

▶ Research the financial signature of several potential bosses to assess their probable valuation trajectory to find the job that will provide you with the best chances for career and financial success.

SELF-DEVELOPMENT EXERCISE

Take the information in this book and apply it to discovering the financial signature of your boss or a prospective boss. Some questions:

What is his or her financial signature?

_____

_____

_____

_____

_____

_____

What is yours?

_____

_____

_____

_____

_____

_____

What is the likely prognosis of your working together?

_____

_____

_____

_____

_____

_____

_____

If it is fairly good, what techniques could you employ that would improve it further?

_____

_____

_____

_____

_____

_____

_____

_____

If it is not good, what techniques could you use to make it better?

_____

_____

_____

_____

_____

_____

_____

_____

_____

ACHIEVING THE FINANCIAL TARGET

The market value improvement process for an enterprise must be far-reaching. It must involve all areas and members of the organization. It needs to be multifaceted, covering strategy, products, and operations as well as finance. It must formally tie the organization together in a common endeavor, namely to improve the long-term financial performance and positioning of the organization.

Market value improvement is not merely a technique. It comes from having the right financial mission aligned correctly with the organization and its strategies. Unlike some conventional approaches, this process is not just restricted to financial parameters. The market value improvement process recognizes that the fundamental driver of company value is people, not financial metrics.

The market value improvement strategy involves four steps, all of which are critical for the company to achieve the optimum market value. These are:

1. Choosing target market value
2. Identifying valuation trajectory and stage

3. Implementing the market value alignment process
4. Implementing the human resources strategy

Choosing Target Market Value

The launching point for the market value improvement process is your company's target market value. Simply choose the market value you want, and then work backward to determine the financial mission required. Work backward from there again to find leaders with this financial mission. In addition, work with your existing leaders to transition their financial missions to the desired ones to support the achievement of the target market value.

In the financial mission model, valuation is elastic. That is, it is infinitely flexible. Naturally, there are practical constraints in the real world. But in principle, your company can achieve whatever market value it desires, relative to its competitors, so long as it is prepared to make the necessary changes to achieve it.

For example, most information technology (IT) consulting enterprises that provide temporary services trade for around 0.5 times revenues. But if they wanted to attract a higher market value—say 1.0 times revenues— they could achieve it. Of course, doing so would require major changes to the financial missions of their leaders. It would probably require that most of their current leadership be removed and replaced with leaders who have different financial missions. Naturally, some leaders would refuse to change their financial missions; without these changes, it would not be possible to achieve the target market value.

If your enterprise is like most, it is not prepared to undergo this amount of change, for a variety of reasons. This puts a practical limit on the target value you can achieve. For the IT consulting company just mentioned, it would more likely set a target market value at 0.75 times revenues. That target would still require changes to the leadership team, but probably not wholesale change.

Leadership and Development

A key function of a company's CEO and its board is to decide on the desired market value outcome of their leadership and then achieve it.

Achieving this goal should not be left to chance. All methods you use to develop and train leaders and their followers should be governed by this goal. Leadership development that is not guided by this overriding market value target is like a cruise missile without a global positioning homing device—it can and will land anywhere. The leadership of the company should be like a laser-guided missile, homing in on the specific target.

Once you understand this perspective, it will permeate all of your leadership strategies. Increasing your individual competencies is useless unless it helps the market value missile home in on its target. First and foremost, leadership training needs to help you achieve your organization's market value target.

Leadership and Return on Investment

The very notion of leadership return on investment (ROI) is irrelevant once there is a target market value.

For example, the ROI for a particular leadership training effort may be positive, however it is measured, but that training's effect on achieving the target market value is negative. Likewise, many leadership actions significantly affect achievement of the target market value, but the resulting ROI is negative. In these cases, the ROI should be rejected, however it is measured, in favor of the target market value.

The problem with using ROI to measure the effect of leadership development is that it is intrinsically the wrong measure. Leadership development is not trying to achieve a positive financial return in the sense of a project-based internal rate of return (IRR) on a leadership development project. That is not the point.

A leadership development project always has a macro-organizational effect. That is why ROI is not the correct measure and why target market value is.

Target market value provides the true ROI measure for leadership effectiveness. Once a target market value has been established, you can measure all of your leadership efforts relative to it. It also helps you answer such questions as: Should the company invest in this new sales program? Should it drop this set of products? Should it acquire this new company? Should it trim this division?

Whether the economic consequences of your actions are soft or hard, you now have a way of looking at them in a consistent manner. The target market value allows you to directly compare the cost of carrying out an effective leadership development program versus investing in a new sales campaign.

Target market value is the vital objective of leadership, the leadership compass that gives you direction. It provides the standard against which you can measure the success of all of your enterprise's activities.

Identifying Valuation Trajectory and Stage

Earlier in the book, we described the nine valuation trajectories and linked them with the nine financial missions. These nine valuation trajectories are essentially primal phases of what may be a complex series of cycles. For the improvement process to work, you need to identify what stage of this cycle you are in.

Once you know where your company is situated, you can identify reasons for this positioning. You can then link your knowledge of your company's position in the market value cycle to the financial missions of its leaders and the leadership team. You can start to develop a market value improvement plan—one that links the leader's particular financial mission to the required market value level, path, and trajectory target.

Implementing the Market Value Alignment Process

The market value improvement process attempts to align the whole organization around the actions required to achieve the target market value. This involves aligning the financial mission of the leaders and followers with the company's strategy and structure. This financial mission needs to support the products and services the company sells and vice versa. This financial mission also needs to be appropriate for the particular stage of evolution in which the company finds itself.

Multifaceted Process

The market value improvement process is depicted in Figure 15.1. As already noted, the market value improvement process is multifaceted—it must take into account the whole organizational ecosystem. People, strategies, and products or services must all be aligned so as to pull in the same direction—the direction required to achieve that target market value.

The market value improvement process is total war. It requires the total commitment of everyone in the organization. Naturally, unless the financial mission of the leaders and the leadership teams are aligned, you have already lost the war. But you must also align the financial mission of the followers; otherwise, they will not be pulling in the same direction. At best, they will unconsciously resist; at worst, they may outright sabotage your efforts. Thus, there must be formal programs for the followers that are every bit as intense as those for the leaders.

Followers must be made aware of the importance of their role. You must show them how to fight alongside of management to achieve the market value target and train them in the techniques they need to succeed. Their inter-

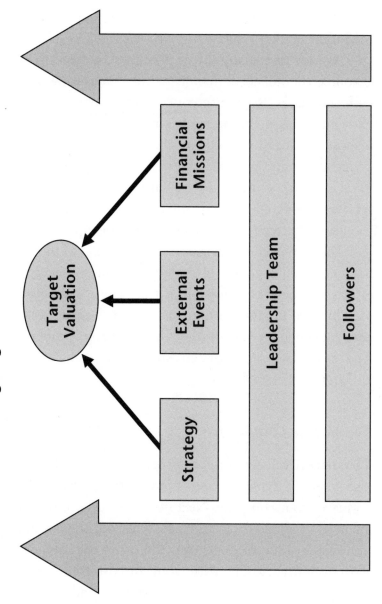

FIGURE 15.1 The valuation targeting model.

ests must be aligned with those of leadership to achieve the target market value.

As part of the alignment process, you need to synchronize the financial missions within your organization with the market structure your company participates in. Whether it is a fragmented, consolidating, or mature market, you need to focus on this aspect for the precise financial mission needed. Likewise, the alignment needs to take into account the particular types of products and services marketed by your organization and the stage of evolution that your company currently occupies.

You also need to pay particular attention to the competencies required by both leaders and followers. In effect, you need to refine all of the competency models used by your organization to ensure that they support the particular market value target the company is pursuing. And, as you will see below, all aspects of human resources will also be affected.

Formalized Approach

The market value alignment process begins with formal assessment of the financial missions of the leaders and followers in your company. Next, it trains them in what the financial missions mean to themselves and the organization and in how to transition their current mission to align it more closely with your organization's needs. Finally, the process moves to coaching individuals as needed to help them become even more effective. However, this process only takes place if leadership has developed a formal market value targeting strategy and a target market value.

In implementing the process, your organization needs to take into account existing strategies, including training and development approaches. None of this will occur with the flick of a switch. You need to have detailed planning in conjunction with the above. But at least you have a road map for implementing the plan. Now the rest is up to your organization.

Implementing the Human Resources Strategy

Your whole organization must be involved in the market value alignment process. But human resources has a particular role to play. In large organizations in particular, human resources should play a role in setting the direction and standards for the human transition required. Such a transition typically includes the following.

Employee Assessment

Knowing the financial signature of your leaders is essential. But knowing the financial signature of your followers, such as employees, is also important. While you probably don't need to study the financial signature of all employees, you would certainly want to look at all those who have an effect on achieving the planned company direction and target market value.

Why would you look at employees' financial missions? In a word, implementation. If your employees' financial missions are not aligned with the target market value, leadership will have problems in implementing the strategy to achieve the target market value. In cases where employees' financial missions are not aligned with that of your company, you can plan appropriate interventions.

Recruitment

Recruitment standards are crucial. If different divisions within your company are hiring employees and executives who have different financial missions, the alignment process will fail.

You need to make executives aware of what they are supposed to be doing and who they are supposed to be hiring. This presumes that they know the company's target market value, the financial mission that best supports the achievement of this goal, and the best way to assess potential employees and interpret the results.

Executives should also know how to apply developmental approaches to employment candidates who do not meet the financial mission requirement. This is bound to happen; fortunately, you can still achieve alignment through a postrecruitment development program.

All of this presumes that your recruiters are trained in selecting the right employees. In implementing the market value improvement process, recruiters—even at the highest levels—also need to be trained in the financial mission model and how this promotes alignment to achieve your company's target market value.

Performance Appraisal and Promotion

Performance appraisals and promotion policies are also essential components of the market value improvement process. Your organization cannot promote an employee unless it knows that her financial mission is aligned with the company's target market value. This implies a formal performance appraisal process. But unlike conventional performance appraisals, it must be formally linked to the target market value through the financial mission.

Each employee needs to be assessed to identify his or her financial signature and mission. Where this leads to a formal development process, you need to have regular, formal monitoring to ensure that alignment with the target market value is proceeding as planned.

If your organization is retrofitting this model, you may need to add prepromotion training and development. In some cases, you may need to add one-on-one coaching with particular employees to help them achieve the financial mission goal. This, of course, implies a cadre of people who are themselves trained in the financial mission model and the target market value required and who are capable of carrying out this type of coaching.

Executive and Leadership Development

Every executive and potential leader of your organization needs to be trained in all aspects of the financial mission model and their role in the alignment process. This will further your objective of achieving alignment among the target market value, leaders, and employees.

Some executives, however, become less open to training over time. For some, their time becomes more valuable and it is more difficult to involve them in training courses. Others develop a sense of hubris and feel that they do not need to be trained. For training for the most senior executives to gain the respect it deserves, it must be tailored to them precisely. They will then quickly see its value and respect the need for the course.

Top executives and leaders often respond negatively to suggestions that they need training. But there will be fewer such leaders if they are shown how this training links directly to the achievement of the target market value through the medium of their own and others' financial mission. This approach also has the benefit of being directly relevant to their own performance goals and, indeed, to their own compensation. This is precisely the sort of incentive you need to ensure that they see such training and development as being worth their valuable time and attention.

Compensation Strategy

Compensation strategy is a crucial issue in the alignment of your organization to its target market value.

Compensation must be linked directly and formally to the achievement of the target market value. For top level employees, you can use a variety of incentives, such as stock options or other equity-related mechanisms. Indeed, many of the legitimate arguments for the use of stock options or other equity-related incentives are actually based on the issue of target market value, even though it is often not couched in those particular terms.

However, one of the major problems in the stock-option debate is that it often takes followers out of the equation. Admittedly, many stock-option plans decline in value. But for most employee-followers, the link between their efforts and the stock price is often, at best, indirect.

Now you can link employees' compensation to other issues that affect target market value directly. One mechanism is training in soft skills to assist in transitioning to the desired financial mission. Another is bonuses for achieving a successful transition to the desired financial mission. Yet another is compensation linked to their success in assisting others in their own financial mission transitions. The list can be extended to any activity, soft or otherwise, that promotes the alignment of the company with the market value improvement process.

Even existing approaches to compensation can be refined and made far more effective by incorporating the concepts and model we have outlined in this book. In effect, their use can be extended by adding on a new approach to aligning compensation strategies with market value objectives.

Training

Implementing the above approaches requires new forms of training. All employees and their leaders need to understand and be trained in this model. This includes selection standards, recruitment approaches, implementation of these approaches, and each person's role in the market value improvement process.

Organizations already have many training programs. But they may need to be modified to be consistent. In many cases, the new model will form a much-needed and valuable refinement to an existing approach. As we have already indicated, for example, traditional competency-based approaches can be refined with the market value targeting model.

Implemented for the first time, the market value targeting model requires training throughout the organization, a key part of the alignment between the market value target and the financial mission of leaders and employees. This training will begin with identifying the financial signature of employees, then will instruct them on the significance of their financial signature and what they need to do, if anything, to transition their financial mission to align it with the organization's target market value.

Human Resources and Financial Mission

The market value targeting model requires a change in behavior on the part of almost everyone in the organization. Some financial signatures will be aligned with the company's financial mission, but most will not.

Behavioral Changes. Market value is about people. If it has not already become obvious, market value is *not* a financial issue; it is a behavioral issue. Much of current business education is based on the assumption that enterprises can achieve market value improvements through financial engineering. That is, through canny manipulation of financial and accounting aggregates, one can increase the market value of an organization.

But that is not the approach we take. In our view, all such financial engineering does is to alter the appearance of the market value of the company without doing anything to alter its substance. We believe that market value improvement starts at the behavioral level. Financial engineering can come later, after the basic behavioral changes have been set in motion.

Responsibility. The responsibility for achieving the financial mission lies with both the CEO and the chief human resources officer, who may well be the CEO himself. More often, this responsibility lies with the CEO in conjunction with the human resources people and the CFO.

The CFO will most certainly be involved. In particular, he will be involved in identifying the most appropriate market value target. Once the behavioral changes have been launched, he will use his responsibility for matters financial to support the company's realignment to the chosen financial mission. He will also warn of any changes needed to the mission and any problems in achieving it.

In essence, the CFO will be the scorekeeper. But the power for this transformation should come at the human level. This will involve the CEO and line managers whose responsibility it is to actually implement human resource strategies.

Guided Market Value: The Task of Leaders

Vision, execution, communication, inspiration—these are the key tasks of leaders. But all of these actions will be for naught if they do not achieve a market value that has positive consequences for shareholders and investors.

Market value is the vital consequence of leadership. It must permeate all thinking on how you direct and manage the leadership process.

Financial signature is the key, the basic matériel from which market value springs. If you ignore financial signature and consequent financial missions, it is at your own peril. Without understanding these chains of causation, you cannot forge a formal path to achieve your desired market value targets.

Your organization must be built around its chosen financial mission to achieve its chosen market value. Your leaders, followers, and strategies must be aligned with the market value target and the common financial mission. This will lead to a shared ethos and financial culture that supports the interests of your shareholders and investors.

If you view the human resource function as merely providing a service for selection and recruitment, your enterprise will fail to achieve its market value mission. All of your leaders must be involved in the human resource function.

Every decision your leaders make must be single-mindedly focused on achieving the market value goal. Every decision is an opportunity to further the financial mission of your company and to achieve its market value target. Every decision leaders make that does not incrementally take them one step nearer to this goal is an opportunity cost to your company in terms of a market value outcome that is less than it would otherwise have been.

Your leaders must judge their staff and their organizations in terms of both opportunities to reach market value goals, and missed opportunities. They should be constantly maximizing the former and reducing the latter.

Your leaders have the awesome responsibility to add to the market value of your enterprise. They must start with the human matériel at their command—the raw financial signatures that lead to your organization's financial mission and market value. They have no excuse not to be able to employ them to good effect.

It is up to you, your leaders, and your organization.

Achieving the Financial Target

This chapter demonstrated that:

▶ The first step in the market value improvement process is identifying the company's target market value.

▶ We must identify the financial missions of leaders and followers to promote alignment between them and the target market value.

▶ We must then identify the valuation trajectory of the company and the stage of the valuation cycle that it is at.

▶ A market value improvement process should be formalized and require all of the organization to be involved.

▶ The success of these programs should be measured by using the concept of target market value.

▶ Both line managers and human resources should be key proponents of the market value improvement process because it is primarily a behavioral, not a financial, issue.

Top Two Takeaways

▶ What do you want the valuation trajectory of your enterprise to be?

▶ Do you and your followers have the right financial mission to achieve this valuation trajectory?

SELF-DEVELOPMENT EXERCISE

Identify a market value target and valuation trajectory for your enterprise.

_____

_____

_____

_____

_____

_____

Identify the financial mission and associated valuation trajectory for each of your top reports.

1. _____

_____

2. _____

_____

3. _____

_____

4. _____

_____

5. _____

_____

Are these missions and trajectories the right ones to achieve your target market value?

_____

_____

_____

_____

_____

_____

Note the top three actions you need to take to align your organization with your target market value and valuation trajectory.

1. _____

_____

2. _____

_____

3. _____

_____

FINANCIAL SIGNATURE SELF-ASSESSMENT

This self-assessment offers you the opportunity to discover whether your financial signature and its resulting financial mission are aligned with the financial mission of your organization.

Note that this assessment is for illustrative purposes only. It is not meant to substitute for a formal assessment of your financial signature or for a formal process of organizational alignment.

Step 1: Your Financial Signature

Review these brief descriptions of the nine financial signature archetypes. Select the signature that comes closest to matching your personal financial preferences, not the style that may be required by your company.

• **Discounter:** a low-expense, low value-adding mission. This represents the very risk-adverse leader who is cash focused, will never speculate, and ensures that his very low gross margins are offset by his extreme thrifti-ness. He focuses on lowering resource use so that it matches the same gross margins. This leader is focused on points of market share and gross margin rather than on dominating the market.

• **Arbitrageur:** a low-expense, medium value-adding mission. This leader is quite focused on return but not so much that she will spend more than the absolute minimum to pursue the opportunity. This leader looks for opportunities carrying relatively decent returns where she can leverage them at a low cost and where she can make profits on the medium-size gross margins she will enjoy.

• **Buccaneer:** a low-expense, high value-adding mission. This leader enjoys very high returns for very low expense—typically, he figures out how to achieve high and ultrahigh returns by means no one has thought of before, so he has few competitors. This is not a leader who will spend many years patiently developing a product or service; he finds opportunities within the limitations of the product, its market, and the company's culture.

• **Trader:** a medium-expense, low value-adding mission that represents a low margin leader. This leader buys cheaply and offers low value-added products, but she uses her wits to make sure that the gross margin always more than offsets the costs of her investment activities. Typically, this leader is in a smaller company that lacks the resources of a big company, and she therefore has to pursue projects without major financial backing and investment.

- **Consolidator:** a medium-expense, medium value-adding mission that represents the leader who adheres to a middle-of-the-road financial mission, a fairly cautious leader. This leader is not a big-picture thinker or strategist but he also shies away from cutthroat low-margin businesses. Neither will he make major investments, making enough to keep gross margins at a just-high-enough level to keep the ship afloat. Typically, this leader consolidates organizationally; productwise, he adds features rather than develops new products.

- **Profiteer:** a medium-expense, high value-adding mission. This leader is essentially an expense-averse Venture Capitalist; she goes for high gross margins but without the high expense tolerated by the Venture Capitalist. She shoots for a lower risk product or service, still with high gross margins. Typically, this leader will aim for product with relatively short development cycles that provide some cash in the short term, even if it means some degradation in the gross margin. But her aim is to make a lot of money using a high gross margin style coupled with medium expenses.

- **Mercantilist:** a high-expense, low value-adding mission. This leader is not focused on product value added but still uses a high level of resources, whether for sales and marketing, for G&A, or even for R&D. He is looking for a way for the high expense levels to lead to company returns without product intensity, usually by increasing market share. Usually, this type of leader is in a large corporate setting where the large investments for such speculative and empire-building activities are available as part of the culture.

- **Conglomerator:** a high-expense, medium value-adding mission. This represents the leader who, as the name implies, has built up a portfolio of products and services, either through internal development or acquisitions, which together meet the medium gross margin characteristics of the style. His product is usually not particularly well differentiated, but it is not a commodity, either.
- **Venture Capitalist:** a high-expense, high value-adding mission that represents the leader who is focused on increasing market share in a significant way. To do this, she tends to use a significant amount of resources. This mission is that of a patient investor who equates a long investment cycle with high returns—as long as the company sticks with the investment, at some stage it will see the high returns from high product value added and hence high earnings.

Step 2: Your Company's Financial Mission

Based on how your organization deploys its resources and its strategies for adding value to the customer experience, select the best description of your company's resource expenditure and value adding:

Resource Expenditure
- **Low:** makes every effort to conserve; budgets are tightly controlled; only the minimum expenditure is used

- **Medium:** willing to make necessary investments in the organization as long as value is created in the short term
- **High:** makes every effort to invest in the building and strengthening of the organization in the short term as well as the long term, even though immediate value may not be realized

Value Adding
- **Low:** offers the minimum quality/variety in products and services needed to assure customer satisfaction
- **Medium:** offers substantial quality and innovation in quality and services that assure a strong competitive position in the market
- **High:** offers the richest possible customer experience, competing for a dominant or preferred position in the market

Select the letter (A through I) in Figure 1 that represents the intersection of the two scores for your organization's resource utilization and value adding.

Step 3: Identifying Financial Mission

In Figure 2, locate both your financial signature from Step 1 and the financial signature of your company from Step 2.

FIGURE 1 Your organization's financial mission.

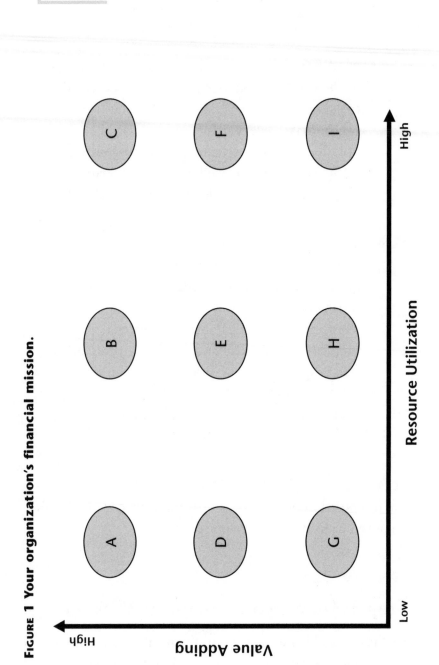

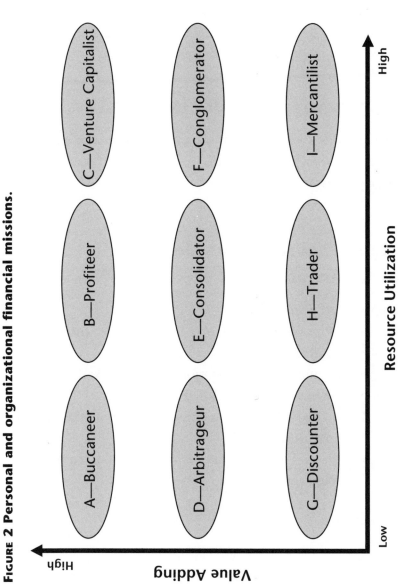

FIGURE 2 Personal and organizational financial missions.

Your Financial Signature _____ (name)
Your Company's Financial Mission
_____ (name)

Step 4: Alignment of Financial Missions

In Figure 3, locate your financial mission in the appropriate diagonal band, then locate the financial mission of your company.

Step 5: Scoring Your Degree of Alignment

Degrees of Separation

0. Both you and your organization have the **same financial mission**.
1. You and your organization occupy the **same band but have different financial styles**.
2. You and your organization are **one financial style separated**.
3. You and your organization are **two financial styles separated**.

Figure 3 Financial mission alignment.

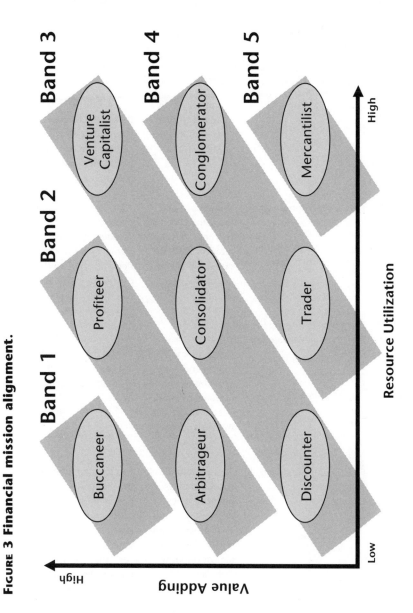

Step 6: Understanding the Mission Alignment Scores

SEPARATION	ALIGNMENT TYPE	SIGNIFICANCE	REQUIRED ACTION
0 (none)	Matched	You are perfectly matched with your organization.	None, but make sure that your organization's financial mission does not change without you becoming aware of it, leaving you high and dry.
1	Congruent	You are not perfectly matched, but you and your organization share the same underlying financial styles.	Your differences are of degree, not substance. You need to make a formal effort to transition your style to that of your organization. You can do this by yourself or with some help.
2	Mismatched	You have a mismatch that will lead to you and your organization having frequent differences in how to achieve market and investment goals.	You need to undertake a formal program of training to overcome this mismatch problem.
3	Conflicted	There is a fundamental clash of financial styles between you and your organization—you are moving in almost opposite directions.	You should either leave the company or undertake a rigorous training program that offers you practical ways to increase your level of alignment such that you will have a minimal level of useful communication.

Step 7: Your Continued Leadership Development

Depending on your score on the self-assessment, you may need different levels of training and intervention. This could include:

- Training for you and your group in how to align financial missions
- A mentor to help you gently transition your mission
- A coach to provide a more focused transition plan
- Training for the organization's managers in how to implement organizational processes that will support and reinforce transitions in the financial missions of its staff

Remember that this exercise is intended to be illustrative only.

To identify your financial signature accurately, contact the Perth Leadership Institute. To find out more information about improving your alignment, contact us at info@perthleadership.org.

INDEX